Savoring Life on the Road

My friends think I'm the luckiest guy on the planet. And who am I to argue?

Sure, it's a tough job traveling to the far ends of the Earth, meeting colorful characters, learning about their culture, having fantastic adventures and sampling some of the world's finest wines, beers and spirits. But hey, somebody's got to do it!

After two years, 20 countries and more than 250 days on the road, I've had ample opportunity to taste how all those wines, beers and spirits are incorporated into some mighty fine meals. And being the nice guy I am, I thought it high time to share some of my favorite dishes with you.

This, my friends, is the result: **Thirsty Traveler-Road Recipes.**

See, if you're lucky like me you learn a thing or two when you're on the road. And one thing I've learned is that no matter where you go, every particular country or region has one wonderful thing in common: great spirits help make great food even better.

Now, if you're not big on booze, don't worry about it! Very few recipes require gallons, quarts, liters or pints of any particular libation. That's the beauty of cooking with wine, beer or spirits generally. Just a little goes a long way. Each adds a subtle but enhancing flavor, taking that dish to an entirely new level of enjoyment.

Variety is the spice of life, right? So look at spirits as a spice. Add that wee dram of 20-year-old single malt Whisky, that vigorous dash of Trinidadian Bitters, that generous splash of French Champagne, or that healthy dollop of Belgian Beer and see what they do to the character of your meal.

Flavor's the key baby. And that's what this book is all about.

So top off your glass, spill a splash where it counts, and prepare to enjoy some fantastically flavorful eats straight from the heart and stomach of the *Thirsty Traveler.*

Welcome to the culinary road less traveled. It's a delicious journey where you'll savor every step.

Are you with me?

Cheers!
-The Thirsty Traveler
(a.k.a. Kevin Brauch)

Publisher: J.W. Ripley
Associate Publisher: Cherene Dyer-Kambeitz
Editor: Bob Poole
Project Coordinator: Joan Moss
Design, Layout and Production by: Acorn Communications Inc.
Cover Photography: Geoff George Photography
Food Photography by: Lisa Preston & John Bilodeau, Bilodeau Preston Ltd.
Additional Photography: Plymouth Gin
                              Inniskillin Winery
                              Mexico Tourism Board
                              Appleton Rum
                              Buffalo Trace Distillery

Props Courtesy of: Linens & Things, The Bay, Downtown, Calgary
Food Stylist: Chef Fred Zimmerman
Food Consultant: Chef Scott Sprouse - Oh Canada Restaurant
Contributors: Michael Bodnarchuk, Kevin Brauch, Susan Cardinal, Cherene Dyer-Kambeitz,
          Linda McGlashan, Dave Wilson, Jim Ripley, Bryan Smith
Web site: www.thirstytraveler.tv

Printed and bound in Canada

Distributed in Canada by White Cap Books Ltd.
351 Lynn Avenue, North Vancouver, British Columbia, Canada V7J 2C4

Distributed in the USA by Graphic Arts Center Publishing Company
3019 N.W. Yeon, Portland, Oregon   97210

National Library of Canada Cataloguing in Publication Data
Ripley, J. W. (James Wilfred), 1955-
    Thirsty Traveler : Road Recipes / J.W. Ripley.
    ISBN 1-55285-566-X
    1. Cookery (Liquors) I. Title.
TX726.R56 2003   641.6'2   C2003-911129-6

Contents

Scotland's Water of Life

For any true Thirsty Traveler, there is one trip – one pilgrimage – that must be made before you die. And that is to the birthplace of William Wallace, Robbie Burns, Bonnie Prince Charlie and the "Water of Life". That place, of course, is Scotland.

The Scot's pride and passion for their famed single malt Whisky is legendary. Originally known as Uisge Beatha or "Water of Life", Uisge became "Us-key" and eventually "Whisky".

From the earliest days of fur-bearing, kilted clansmen waging war against each other and their oppressors, the Scottish have always fought for what they believed in. Like the right to distill their own "Water of Life". Heavily taxed by government, Scottish distillers took to making Whisky in secret underground stills, and over the course of hundreds of years perfected their techniques.

Man am I ever glad they did. The heavenly tastes of single malt are as varied as the Scottish landscape. Highland Whisky is rich, mellow and sometimes sweet especially when aged in sherry casks instead of the more common bourbon casks.

Contrast Highland Whisky to those from the island of Islay (pronounced eye'-la).

For hundreds of years, this craggy jewel known as the "Queen of the Hebrides" has produced world-famous Whisky with a very distinctive taste. See, on Islay they have no shortage of water and no shortage of peat. Peat is used here to heat homes and to dry the precious malt for making their Whisky.

Take it from the Thirsty Traveler – this is not a Whisky for the faint of heart! Islay Whisky is strong, distinct and very peaty. It's these unique characteristics that make Islay Whiskies stand out on the world stage of Scotch. They also stand out in the kitchen, too.

Just imagine a nice freshly caught salmon, smoked and soaked in Islay's finest single malt Whisky. Then there's Scotland's famous Black Angus beef, even more delicious when served in a black peppercorn whisky sauce. Aye, that's good eating, indeed!

It's high time for a wee dram. So raise your glass and join me in a hearty Slainte – or good health – to Scotland and its wonderful, wonderful Whisky!

A toast to Urquhart Castle on the shores of ▶ Scotland's legendary Loch Ness.

Honey Glazed
Chicken Risotto

things you need...

4 x 5 oz	*(130 g)*	chicken fillets
2 Tbsp	*(30 ml)*	olive oil
3 Tbsp	*(45 ml)*	**Whisky**
2 Tbsp	*(30 ml)*	grain mustard
3½ Tbsp	*(50 ml)*	honey
3 Tbsp	*(45 ml)*	onion, finely chopped
1½ Tbsp	*(20 ml)*	butter
½ cup	*(120 ml)*	mushrooms, sliced
1		garlic clove, finely chopped
½ cup	*(120 ml)*	cooked risotto (boiled in water and drained)
1 cup	*(240ml)*	chicken stock, canned
1 cup	*(240 ml)*	whipping cream
3 Tbsp	*(45 ml)*	parmesan cheese, fresh, grated
2 Tbsp	*(30 ml)*	parsley, chopped
		salt and pepper to taste

...now get cookin'

Preheat oven to 350°F *(175°C)*.

In a frying pan, brown the chicken fillets in olive oil until half cooked on both sides. Place on a roasting tray.

Deglaze the frying pan the chicken was cooked in by adding **Whisky**. Reduce by half.

Once reduced, add the grain mustard and honey to frying pan. Mix well and pour most of the glaze over the chicken in roasting tray. Save a portion of the glaze. Place in the oven.

In a heavy-bottomed saucepan, fry the onion in the butter, and then add the mushrooms and garlic. Cook through for a few minutes.

Add the cooked risotto and mix.

Add the stock and cook gently, stirring constantly. Cook for approximately 5 minutes.

Add the cream and cook further until a creamy consistency is achieved.

Add the parmesan and the parsley. Season with salt and pepper.

Remove chicken from the oven and put to one side.

Place risotto on a plate. Cut the chicken into 2 pieces and place on top of the risotto. Drizzle the remaining honey and mustard glaze on top. Serve immediately.

Serves 4

The word Whiskey, with an 'e' is how the generic word is spelled when unconnected to a specific brand. Most American and Irish distillers use this spelling where as Scottish and Candian distillers drop the 'e' as in Whisky.

Whisky
Pepper Steak

things you need...

Sauce

2 Tbsp	*(30 ml)*	white onion, chopped
1 Tbsp	*(15 ml)*	butter
2 cups	*(480 ml)*	beef stock or canned beef broth
¼ tsp	*(1 ml)*	black pepper, cracked
1		garlic clove, pressed
2 Tbsp	*(30 ml)*	**Whisky**
1		green onion, chopped
1 tsp	*(5 ml)*	cornstarch
1 Tbsp	*(15 ml)*	water

Pepper Steak

1 lb	*(450 g)*	sirloin steak, cut into two portions
2 tsp	*(10 ml)*	black pepper, cracked
2 Tbsp	*(30 ml)*	butter
		salt to taste

Roaming Highland cattle are an unusual traffic hazard on Islay.

...now get cookin'

Fire up the BBQ.

To make the sauce: In a saucepan, sauté the white onions in butter over high heat until the onions turn brown.

Add 1 cup *(240 ml)* of the beef stock, cracked black pepper and garlic. Continue to simmer over medium high heat until the sauce has reduced by about half.

Add **Whisky**, green onion and remaining cup of beef stock to the sauce and let it simmer over low heat while you prepare the steaks.

Spread ½ tsp *(2 ml)* of cracked pepper over the entire surface of each side of the sirloin steaks and press it into the steaks so that it sticks.

Melt 2 Tbsp *(30 ml)* of butter in a large skillet over medium high heat. Drop the steaks into the melted butter and sear each side of the steaks for 1½ to 2 minutes or until brown.

On a hot BBQ, grill the steaks for 3 to 5 minutes per side or until they are done to your liking. Salt the steaks lightly as they grill.

When the steaks are just about done, combine the cornstarch with the Tbsp *(15 ml)* of water in a small bowl. Stir just until the cornstarch dissolves.

Remove the whisky sauce from the heat and add the cornstarch to it.

Put the sauce back on the heat and continue to cook on low until the sauce is thickened to a gravy consistency.

Pour sauce over your steaks and serve.

Serves 2

The hallowed Scotch Malt Whisky Society fittingly meets in one of Edinburgh's oldest buildings, the Vaults in Leith, at the corner of Henderson Street and Giles Street.

Sips & Tips
the Thirsty Traveler

Whisky
Green Beans

Highland
Whisky Fondue

things you need...

1 lb	(450 g)	green beans, fresh
		salt to taste
1		portobello mushroom cap, cubed
⅓ cup	(80 ml)	onion, coarsely chopped
1		garlic clove, crushed
½ tsp	(3 ml)	thyme
1 Tbsp	(15 ml)	butter
1 Tbsp	(15 ml)	flour
¼ cup	(60 ml)	water
¼ cup	(60 ml)	light cream
3 Tbsp	(45 ml)	**Whisky**
¼ cup	(60 ml)	slivered almonds

...now get cookin'

Trim ends of beans and cut in halves. Boil the beans in salted water just until tender.

In a saucepan, sauté mushroom, onions, garlic and thyme in butter until tender. Stir in flour.

In a small bowl, mix water and cream together, then add to mushroom and onion mixture in saucepan. Cook, stirring constantly, until mixture thickens.

Stir in **Whisky**, and add cooked green beans. Continue to heat until warmed through.

Garnish individual servings with slivered almonds.

Serves 6

things you need...

1		onion, small, finely chopped
1 Tbsp	(15 ml)	butter
1 cup	(240 ml)	milk
2 cups	(480 ml)	Scottish or mature cheddar cheese, grated
1 Tbsp	(15 ml)	corn flour
4 Tbsp	(60 ml)	**Whisky**
1 loaf		rye bread, cubed
1 loaf		onion bread, cubed for dipping
		thyme, fresh for garnish
1		baguette, fresh or toasted, sliced

...now get cookin'

Put onion and butter into a saucepan and cook over a gentle heat until soft.

Add milk and heat until bubbling.

Gradually stir in cheese and continue to cook until melted, stirring frequently.

In a small bowl, blend corn flour smoothly with **Whisky**.

Stir Whisky mixture into cheese mixture and cook 2 to 3 minutes until thickened, stirring frequently.

Pour into the fondue pot and serve with cubes of rye and onion bread.

Garnish fondue with fresh thyme and chunks of cheddar.

Serves 4 to 6 ***(facing page)***

The Queen of the Hebridean Islands, Islay (pronounced eye-la), is only 25 miles long and 20 miles wide, yet has more than half-a-dozen distilleries.

Wicked
Whisky Balls

Scottish
Yams

things you need...

1 cup	*(240 ml)*	pecans, ground
1 cup	*(240 ml)*	chocolate wafer cookie crumbs, ground
1 cup	*(240 ml)*	icing sugar
1½ Tbsp	*(22 ml)*	light corn syrup
¼ cup	*(60 ml)*	**Whisky**
		icing sugar for rolling

things you need...

2½ cups	*(600 ml)*	yams, cooked, mashed
4 Tbsp	*(60 ml)*	butter, softened
½ cup	*(120 ml)*	sugar, light brown, firmly packed
		salt to taste
⅓ cup	*(80 ml)*	**Whisky**
		pecan halves or mini marshmallows for topping

...now get cookin'

Mix ground pecans and chocolate wafers together, and empty into a large bowl.

Mix in the sugar, corn syrup and **Whisky** very thoroughly (use your hands).

Shape the mixture into balls the size of a quarter and roll in icing sugar.

Keep in an airtight container in a cool place, or freeze on a baking sheet until each ball is firm.
Store in tightly sealed plastic bags.

Makes 2 to 3 dozen

...now get cookin'

Preheat oven to 325°F *(160°C.)*.

In a large mixing bowl, combine all ingredients except topping.

Spoon into a greased 4 cup *(945 ml)* casserole dish.

Top with pecan halves and/or mini marshmallows. Bake for 20 to 25 minutes until bubbly.

Serves 6 to 8   ***(facing page)***

A castle maintains a lonely vigil off Scotland's west coast.

Sips & Tips
the Thirsty Traveler

To test the age of Whisky, place a few drops on your tongue for five seconds. You'll feel the heat of a younger spirit on the tip of your tongue, a 16-year-old at the middle, a 20-year-old at the back. Anything older, you'll feel the heat in your chest.

Mexico's Gift from the Gods

Hola! There's a whole lot more to Tequila than meets the eye. Above ground, and below ground, too!

This fine spirit takes its name from the town of Tequila, which is at the epi-center of Mexico's Tequila industry. Located just north of Gaudalajara, this place is high. At 5,000 feet above sea level, we're talking way up there. The mile-high altitude and torrid daytime temperatures make ideal growing conditions for the blue agave - the source material for Tequila's fiery bite.

Persuading Mother Nature to give up her blue agave can be back-breaking work. These guys typically weigh in at 50 pounds. And the biggest ones can even tip the scales at 175 pounds! Try digging up one of those bad boys in the midday sun. Aye, carumba!

Tequila evolved from an ancient drink originally made by the Aztecs. Legend has it that a bolt of lightning struck a blue agave field and tore into the heart of one of the plants, burning a hole and cooking bits of the plant's innards. After these charred bits started to ferment, the natives noticed nectar oozing out of the plant.

Just like the Thirsty Traveler, the Aztecs couldn't resist trying it. One sip and the mysterious nectar was promptly dubbed, "A Gift from the Gods." A few hundred years later when the Spanish Conquistadors swept across Mexico, the art of distillation was introduced and soon Aztec nectar became Tequila as we know it today.

True Tequila is made from the heart, or piña, of the blue agave, a plant that can take a dozen years to grow. That's one reason why the high-end stuff can be very expensive. Premium Tequila is made from 100% blue agave. If it does not boast that on the label, then it is a mixto, a blend with only 51% blue agave. Tequila can be drunk right out of the vat, though some premium brands are barrel-aged for up to six years.

Fine Tequila is a wonderful sipping drink. It's also a fabulous addition to any adventurous chef's tool chest. Imagine freshly-caught shrimp, pan-seared with butter and newly-picked herbs, then flambéed with 100% blue agave Tequila. Or Tequila lime swordfish! Or shrimp tacos with salsa! Mmmm … Delicioso? Muy, my friends, muy.

A spectacular blue agave field near ▶ Tequila, Mexico.

Shrimp Taco
with Salsa

things you need...

1 lb	*(450 g)*	shrimp, medium or large, peeled, deveined
3 Tbsp	*(45 ml)*	**Tequila**
¼ cup	*(60 ml)*	lime juice, freshly squeezed
¼ tsp	*(1 ml)*	salt
¼ tsp	*(1 ml)*	cayenne pepper
2		avocados, diced
2		tomatoes, medium, diced
1 cup	*(240 ml)*	cilantro leaves, fresh, chopped
¼ cup	*(60 ml)*	red onion, diced
¼ cup	*(60 ml)*	lime juice, freshly squeezed
¼ tsp	*(1 ml)*	salt
¼ tsp	*(1 ml)*	black pepper, freshly ground
8		taco shells

...now get cookin'

Preheat oven to 350°F *(175ºC)*.

In a bowl, combine shrimp, **Tequila**, lime juice, salt and cayenne pepper. Toss, cover and allow to sit at room temperature for ½ hour.

In a second bowl, add avocados, tomatoes, cilantro, onion, lime juice, salt and pepper. Toss gently, do not mash avocado.

Warm taco shells for 4 minutes.

Drain off shrimp marinade. Discard. On a grill, or in a skillet over medium-high heat, cook shrimp for approximately 1 minute per side, or until all pink disappears.

To serve, spoon avocado salsa into taco shells. Top with shrimp.

Serves 4

Fiesta
Wings

things you need...

2 lbs	*(1 kg)*	chicken wings, drumettes
½ cup	*(120 ml)*	**Tequila, Gold**
¼ cup	*(60 ml)*	orange juice, frozen, concentrate
1		lemon zest
¼ cup	*(60 ml)*	lemon juice, freshly squeezed
2		garlic cloves, minced
½ tsp	*(2 ml)*	cumin, ground
1 tsp	*(5 ml)*	black pepper, freshly ground
1 tsp	*(5 ml)*	salt
2 Tbsp	*(30 ml)*	cilantro leaves, fresh, minced

...now get cookin'

Wash the wings, pat dry and place in a large, heavy-duty resealable plastic food bag.

In a small bowl, combine the remaining ingredients. Pour the marinade over the wings in the bag. Seal the bag and refrigerate several hours or overnight.

Prepare a medium-hot charcoal fire or preheat a gas grill to medium-high.

Drain the wings, discarding the marinade.

Grill the wings, turning often, until they are slightly charred and cooked through, about 25 minutes.

Serves 4 **(see facing page)**

During the annual Tequila carnival and parade, producers hand out small bottles of Tequila to the crowd lining the streets.

Shrimp
Salad Arriba

things you need...

2 Tbsp	*(30 ml)*	cilantro, fresh, chopped
2		garlic cloves, minced
1		serrano chili, stemmed, seeded, finely diced
½ cup	*(120 ml)*	**Tequila**
2 Tbsp	*(30 ml)*	**Triple Sec** or **Grand Marnier**
¼ cup	*(60 ml)*	lime juice, freshly squeezed
1 tsp	*(5 ml)*	cumin seed, toasted or ground
1 lb	*(450 g)*	shrimp (16 to 20), peeled, deveined
¼ cup	*(60 ml)*	olive oil
		salt and pepper to taste
4 x 6"	*(15 cm)*	corn tortillas, cut into julienne strips
½ cup	*(120 ml)*	vegetable oil
1 tsp	*(5 ml)*	chili powder
1		tomato, cored, seeded, diced
1		yellow bell pepper, cored, seeded, diced
6 cups	*(1.4 L)*	romaine lettuce leaves, washed thoroughly, dried

...now get cookin'

Combine the cilantro, garlic, chili, **Tequila**, **Triple Sec**, lime juice and cumin in a bowl. Add the shrimp, turn to coat, and refrigerate for at least 1 hour. Drain the shrimp and reserve the marinade.

In a small saucepan and over high heat, bring the reserved marinade to a boil. Reduce the heat to medium and simmer until reduced by half. Remove from the heat, transfer to a bowl, and let cool. Whisk in the olive oil and season with salt and pepper. Set aside.

Heat a fry pan on medium-high with 2 Tbsp *(30ml)* vegetable oil. Cook the shrimp until just pink, about 1 minute per side. Add salt and pepper. Keep warm.

Fill a small skillet with oil to a depth of about 1" *(2.5 cm)* and place over medium heat. When the oil is hot, fry the tortilla strips in batches until light brown and crisp. Drain on paper towels. Sprinkle with chili powder while still warm.

In a large bowl, mix together the tomato, pepper and lettuce. Toss with the marinade-oil dressing and divide among 4 large plates or shallow bowls. Top the salad with grilled shrimp and fried tortilla strips. Serve immediately.

Serves 4

Some say Tequila means 'the rock that cuts', so named for the black obsidian rock that surrounds the town.

Fettuccini
Chicken with Tequila

things you need...

⅓ **cup**	*(80 ml)*	cilantro, fresh, chopped
2 Tbsp	*(30 ml)*	garlic, minced
2 Tbsp	*(30 ml)*	jalapeno peppers, minced
4 Tbsp	*(60 ml)*	butter, unsalted
½ **cup**	*(120 ml)*	chicken stock
¼ **cup**	*(60 ml)*	**Tequila**
2 Tbsp	*(30 ml)*	lime juice, freshly squeezed
3 Tbsp	*(45 ml)*	soy sauce, low salt
1¼ lbs	*(560 g)*	chicken breast, skinless, cut into ½" *(1 cm)* strips
¼ **cup**	*(60 ml)*	red onion, sliced
1		red bell pepper, thinly sliced
½		yellow bell pepper, thinly sliced
½		green bell pepper, thinly sliced
16 oz	*(450 g)*	fettuccini pasta
1½ cups	*(360 ml)*	whipping cream

Dancing girls from Oaxaca balance baskets of flowers on their heads.

...now get cookin'

In a medium saucepan, sauté the cilantro, garlic and jalapeno pepper in 2 Tbsp *(30 ml)* of butter over medium heat for 4 to 5 minutes. Add the stock, **Tequila** and lime juice. Bring the mixture to a boil and cook until reduced to a paste-like consistency. Set aside.

Pour soy sauce over the chicken and set aside for 5 minutes.

Meanwhile, in a medium sized skillet, sauté the onion and peppers with the remaining 2 Tbsp *(30 ml)* butter, stirring occasionally.

Cook fettuccini according to package directions.

When the peppers have wilted, add the chicken and soy sauce. Toss and add the reserved Tequila/lime paste and cream. Bring to a boil. Gently simmer until the chicken is cooked through and sauce is thick. Toss with well drained fettuccini and garnish with cilantro.

Serves 4

Sorry to destroy the myth, but bottles of Tequila do not have a worm in them, you must be thinking of Mezcal.

Sips & Tips
the Thirsty Traveler

Mexican
Beef Stew

things you need...

¼ **cup**	(60 ml)	vegetable oil
2 lbs	(1 kg)	beef (boneless chuck, tip or round), cut into 1" (2.5 cm) cubes
½ **cup**	(120 ml)	onion, chopped
6		bacon slices, cut into 1" (2.5 cm) pieces
¼ **cup**	(60 ml)	carrots, chopped
¼ **cup**	(60 ml)	celery, chopped
¼ **cup**	(60 ml)	**Tequila**
¼ **cup**	(175 ml)	tomato juice
2 Tbsp	(30 ml)	cilantro, fresh, chopped
¼ **cup**	(60 ml)	flour, all purpose
1½ **tsp**	(7 ml)	salt
15 oz	(425 g)	garbanzo beans, canned
1½ **cups**	(360 ml)	tomatoes, chopped,
2		garlic cloves, finely chopped

...now get cookin'

Heat the oil in 10" (25 cm) skillet until hot. Stir beef in oil over medium heat for a least 1 hour. Remove beef with slotted spoon and drain.

Cook and stir the onion and bacon in same skillet until bacon is crisp.

Stir in beef and remaining ingredients. Heat to boiling then reduce the heat to medium low. Cover and simmer until beef is tender, about 1 hour.

Serves 6 to 8

Thirsty
Shrimp

things you need...

½		onion, large, finely diced
10		shallots, finely diced
1		red bell pepper, large, chopped
3 Tbsp	(45 ml)	butter
2 lbs	(1 kg)	shrimp, peeled, deveined
6 Tbsp	(90 ml)	parsley, fresh, chopped
2 Tbsp	(30 ml)	capers, chopped
¼ **tsp**	(1 ml)	celery salt
½ **cup**	(120 ml)	**Tequila**
		salt and pepper to taste

...now get cookin'

Using butter, sauté the onion, shallots and pepper. Add the shrimp and cook shrimp until pink in color.

Add the parsley, capers, celery salt and 1 cup (240 ml) of **Tequila** to pan. Season with salt and pepper.

When ready to serve, flambé with remaining **Tequila**.

Serves 6   **(facing page)**

Tequila is made from the blue agave plant. This cactus-like plant takes up to 12 years to reach the level of maturity necessary to produce Tequila.

Tequila
Lime Swordfish

things you need...

| 2 | | swordfish steaks, 2" *(5 cm)* thick (you can substitute shark or tuna) |

Marinade #1

¼ cup	*(60 ml)*	**Tequila**
¼ tsp	*(1 ml)*	onion powder
½ tsp	*(2 ml)*	orange peel, grated
3 Tbsp	*(45 ml)*	lime juice, freshly squeezed
1 tsp	*(5 ml)*	olive oil
¼ tsp	*(1 ml)*	paprika

Marinade #2
Same ingredients as above, plus

| 3 Tbsp | *(45 ml)* | sour cream, nonfat |

...now get cookin'

In a bowl, stir in the **Tequila**, onion powder, orange peel, lime juice, olive oil, and paprika. Rinse the fish and turn in mixture. Cover and chill from 10 minutes to 2 hours.

Make a second marinade and set aside.

Remove fish and add left-over marinade#1 to second batch of marinade. Grill fish over medium coals until lightly browned, about 10 to 14 minutes. Remove and keep warm.

Heat the marinade in a pan to boiling. Remove from heat and whisk in sour cream until it reaches a sauce consistency. Spoon over fish and serve with a side of rice or vegetables.

Serves 2

Awe-inspiring cathedral in San Miguel de Allende, Mexico.

Entertainers Jimmy Buffett and Sammy Hagar have their own signature brands of Tequila.

Cold Lime
and Cucumber Soup

things you need...

2		limes, zested
⅓ cup	(80 ml)	lime juice, freshly squeezed
¼ cup	(60 ml)	jalapeno pepper, seeded, chopped
2		cucumbers, large, peeled, chopped
2 cups	(480 ml)	green grapes, seedless
4		green onions, chopped
¼ cup	(60 ml)	cilantro, fresh, chopped
½ cup	(120 ml)	orange or yellow bell pepper, chopped
⅓ cup	(80 ml)	**Tequila**
		cucumber and green onions, finely minced

...now get cookin'

Put all of the ingredients, except the **Tequila** and the garnish, in a blender. Pureé everything until smooth. Then press through a sieve.

Chill in the refrigerator until ready to serve.

Stir in the **Tequila**, ladle into bowls, and sprinkle each with the cucumber and green onion.

Serves 2

Siesta
Sorbet

things you need...

1 cup	(240 ml)	lime juice
1 Tbsp	(15 ml)	lime rind, finely grated
1¼ cups	(300 ml)	sugar
3 cups	(710 ml)	grapefruit juice, ruby, bottled
⅓ cup	(90 ml)	**Tequila**
1		mint sprig

...now get cookin'

Place lime juice, lime rind and sugar in a saucepan. Stir mixture over low heat until sugar has dissolved.

Pour grapefruit juice, sugar mixture and **Tequila** into a bowl. Stir to combine.

Pour mixture into a freezer proof bowl and freeze for 1 hour.

Whisk sorbet and freeze for another hour.

Whisk sorbet again and freeze until solid.

Garnish with a sprig of mint and serve.

Serves 6

Owners of the prized blue agave plant will patrol their precious fields to protect them from poachers and rustlers.

Grape Beginnings in Sonoma

Sonoma County is bordered by its more famous neighbor, the Napa Valley, to the east and the Pacific Ocean to the west. The County straddles mountains and valleys – and a booming Wine industry.

Father Jose Altamira gets credit for planting the first vineyards here back in the 1820s. His grapes were soon dubbed the Mission grapes. They basically sucked as far as making good Wine goes. But hey, they were a beginning – a grape beginning!

From one end of Sonoma County to the other, you'll find vineyard after vineyard, even on the coast people will tell you that the Pacific Ocean is the industry's best friend. It brings fog and rain – but it also adds flavor.

Along the coast, the trick is to find a slope that catches the sun but which is also above the fog line. Apparently, the cool morning fog and air coupled with the warm afternoon sun, allows the vines to mature slowly, creating a rich mature fruit.

While most of the grape varieties grown in the United States can be traced back to European ancestors, Zinfandel is the only grape that experts feel is truly American. All that grafting of young grape buds to the old vines way back when seems to have created a unique American grape.

Ever the trend-setters, Californians are always among the first to experiment and implement new ways of cooking. And with Sonoma definitely at the top of its class, many of San Francisco's better bistros come here to shop for top-quality groceries – including, of course, the County's wonderful Wines.

Sonoma is also renowned for its cheeses. Not sure where to start? Go visit Vella – one of the region's top cheese shops – and they'll be delighted to help you forage for fromage. No picnic basket would be complete without some tasty Sonoma Jack cheese and a bottle of Zin (for Zinfandel – dude, this is California!) or Chardonnay. Or perhaps a wheel of nutty-sweet Dry Jack paired with a Pinot Noir. Now, find a cozy hilltop overlooking a Pacific sunset and, man, you are in oenophile heaven.

It's no stretch to say that Sonoma is destined for grape greatness. So who'll drink to that? You guessed it – the Thirsty Traveler, that's who!

**The Thirsty Traveler samples the merchandise ▶
at a vineyard near Cazadero, California.**

Mama Mia
Marinated Mushrooms

things you need...

½ **cup**	*(120 ml)*	olive oil, extra virgin
4		garlic cloves, halved lengthwise, roasted
2 lbs	*(1 kg)*	mushrooms, small, stems trimmed
½ **cup**	*(120 ml)*	parsley, fresh, chopped
1½ cups	*(360 ml)*	**White Wine, dry**
¼ **cup**	*(60 ml)*	lemon juice, freshly squeezed
2 Tbsp	*(30 ml)*	red wine vinegar
6		cloves, whole
2		bay leaves
1 tsp	*(4 ml)*	red pepper flakes
		garnish with lemon zest
		salt and pepper to taste

...now get cookin'

Heat the oil in heavy large skillet over medium-low heat. Add the garlic and sauté until golden. Discard the garlic. Increase heat to medium-high. Add the mushrooms and parsley, sauté until mushrooms are golden.

Reduce heat to medium-low and stir in remaining ingredients.

Cover and simmer for 5 minutes. Season with salt and pepper. Cool to room temperature. Transfer to container, cover and chill until cold. (Can be made 2 days ahead.) Keep chilled. Drain mushrooms before serving and garnish with lemon zest.

Serves 12 **(facing page)**

Time out on a beach not far from Bodega Bay, California.

Sips & Tips

the Thirsty Traveler

The U.S. is the 4th largest Wine-producing nation in the world, trailing only Italy, France and Spain.

California
Crab Dip

things you need...

1		leek, medium, white part only, chopped
½ cup	(120 ml)	spinach, frozen, thawed, chopped
1		sweet onion, medium, finely chopped
2 Tbsp	(30 ml)	garlic, minced
2 Tbsp	(30 ml)	olive oil
½ cup	(120 ml)	artichoke hearts, canned, drained, chopped
¼ cup	(60 ml)	**White Wine**
⅔ cup	(160 ml)	whipping cream
1 lb	(450 g)	Brie, cut into ¼" (6 mm) pieces

3 tsp	(15 ml)	parsley leaves, fresh, finely chopped
2 Tbsp	(30 ml)	dill leaves, fresh, finely chopped
1 Tbsp	(15 ml)	tarragon leaves, fresh, finely chopped
1 lb	(450 g)	crab meat, fresh
2 Tbsp	(30 ml)	Dijon mustard
1 tsp	(5 ml)	tabasco
		salt and pepper to taste
		baguette slices, toasted

...now get cookin'

Preheat oven to 425°F *(220°C).*

Lightly oil a 6 cup *(1.5 L)* shallow baking dish.

Wash leek well and drain. Squeeze and dry the spinach.

In a heavy skillet, cook leek, onion and garlic in oil over moderate heat, stirring, until pale golden. Stir in the artichoke hearts and spinach. Add **White Wine** and cook, stirring, 3 minutes. Add cream and simmer, stirring, 1 minute. Add Brie, stirring until it just begins to melt. Remove skillet from heat and stir parsley, dill and tarragon into mixture.

In a large bowl, stir together crab, mustard, tabasco, and salt and pepper and stir in cheese mixture. Spread mixture evenly in baking dish and bake in middle of oven 15 to 20 minutes, or until golden.

Serve dip hot with toasted baguette.

Serves 6 to 8

Our Thirsty crew at the Golden Gate Bridge, San Francisco.

Sips & Tips
the Thirsty Traveler

In the mid 1800s, Hungarian Count Agoston Haraszthy brought 100,000 vine cuttings from Europe to Sonoma. He is known as the father of the California Wine industry.

American
Potato Salad

things you need...

¼ cup	*(60 ml)*	chicken broth, canned, low salt
¼ cup	*(60 ml)*	**White Wine, dry**
¼ cup	*(60 ml)*	olive oil, extra virgin
4		green onions, chopped
2 Tbsp	*(30 ml)*	Dijon mustard
2 Tbsp	*(30 ml)*	white wine vinegar
2 Tbsp	*(30 ml)*	capers, drained
3¼ lbs	*(1.5 kg)*	red-skinned potatoes, washed, cubed

...now get cookin'

Whisk first seven ingredients in large bowl to blend and season with salt and pepper to taste. Cover and refrigerate. (Can be prepared 1 day ahead. Bring to room temperature before continuing.)

Cook the potatoes in large pot of boiling salted water until just tender, about 25 minutes. Drain. Return potatoes to pot. Place pot over low heat until liquid from potatoes evaporates, about 2 minutes.

Add dressing to warm potatoes and toss gently to coat. Let stand at least 1 hour at room temperature. Toss again and serve.

Serves 8

Sinatra's
Italian Pasta Salad

things you need...

¾ lb	*(340 g)*	Italian sausage, casings removed
2 Tbsp	*(30 ml)*	olive oil
1 cup	*(240 ml)*	white onion, chopped
4		garlic cloves, large finely chopped
3 cups	*(710 ml)*	broccoli florets
1		zucchini, medium, chopped
¼ cup	*(60 ml)*	**White Wine, dry**
5		tomatoes, large plum, seeded, diced
1 lb	*(450 g)*	rotini or fusilli pasta, freshly cooked
1 cup	*(240 ml)*	parmesan cheese, freshly grated
½ cup	*(120 ml)*	black olives, drained, cut in half
½ cup	*(120 ml)*	parmesan cheese salad dressing (purchased)
		salt and pepper to taste

...now get cookin'

Sauté sausage in heavy large skillet over medium heat until cooked through, breaking up with spoon, about 6 minutes. Using a slotted spoon, transfer the sausage to paper towels. Pour off drippings and add oil to same skillet.

Add the onion and garlic, sauté until translucent, about 5 minutes. Add broccoli, zucchini and **White Wine**, sauté until vegetables are just tender, about 4 minutes. Add the sausage and tomatoes, toss until heated through, about 2 minutes.

Transfer to a large bowl. Add pasta, cheese, olives and enough dressing to coat the mixture. Season with salt and pepper.

Serves 4

Sonoma has over 40,000 acres of vineyards, and crushes over 113,000 tons of grapes per year.

Turkey Tacos
and Red Pepper Salsa

things you need...

1 Tbsp	*(15 ml)*	canola oil
2 lbs	*(1 kg)*	turkey cutlets, cut into ¾" *(2 cm)* strips
2½ tsp	*(12 ml)*	cumin, ground
½ tsp	*(2 ml)*	cayenne pepper
		salt to taste
⅓ cup	*(80 ml)*	**White Wine, dry**
7 oz	*(200 g)*	red bell peppers, roasted (in the jar or fresh roasted)
4 oz	*(115 g)*	red onion, quartered
½ cup	*(120 ml)*	cilantro leaves, fresh, well packed
½		lime, fresh
1 cup	*(240 ml)*	sour cream, low fat or plain yogurt, low fat
12 x 6"	*(15 cm)*	flour tortillas
1		bunch watercress lettuce, washed, spun dry

...now get cookin'

Heat the canola oil in a nonstick skillet over medium heat. Add the turkey and increase the heat to high. Season with cumin, cayenne pepper and salt. Stir for 2 minutes.

Add the **White Wine**. Cook, stirring periodically, until almost all the liquid evaporates, about 3 minutes.

Drain the roasted peppers in a small colander. Put the roasted peppers, onion and cilantro leaves in a food processor. Pulse until coarsely chopped. Juice the lime half and add to the food processor with salt to taste. Pulse until well combined but still slightly chunky. Put into a serving bowl.

Spread the tortillas on a microwave safe plate and cover with a paper towel. Cook in a microwave oven on high power for 20 seconds. Meanwhile, spoon the cooked turkey onto a platter. Put the sour cream in a small serving bowl.

To assemble a taco, lay a tortilla flat and put a few sprigs of watercress down the center. Then add 1 to 2 oz *(30 to 60 g)* of turkey, 1 Tbsp *(15 ml)* of sour cream and 1 Tbsp *(15 ml)* of salsa. Do not overfill. Fold and serve.

Makes 3 tacos per person.

Serves 4 **(facing page)**

When choosing Wine for a meal, look for a match between the flavor characteristics of the food and Wine. Lighter flavored Wines usually go better with lighter flavored dishes and robust Wines with robust foods.

Creamy
Pork Medallions

things you need...

1 lb	*(450 g)*	pork tenderloin, cut crosswise in ½" *(1 cm)* thick pieces
⅓ cup	*(80 ml)*	flour, all purpose
½ tsp	*(2 ml)*	salt
¼ tsp	*(1 ml)*	black pepper, freshly ground
3 Tbsp	*(45 ml)*	butter
3		green onions, diced, white and green parts separated
½ cup	*(120 ml)*	**White Wine, dry**
1 cup	*(240 ml)*	whipping cream
¼ cup	*(60 ml)*	Dijon mustard

...now get cookin'

Pound the tenderloin between sheets of waxed paper to the thickness of ¼" *(5 mm)*.

Combine flour, salt and pepper in shallow dish.

Melt 1 Tbsp *(15 ml)* butter in heavy large skillet over medium-high heat.

Dredge pork in seasoned flour, shaking off excess. Add ⅓ of pork to skillet and sauté until brown and cooked through, about 2 minutes per side. Transfer to platter and keep warm. Repeat with remaining pork in 2 more batches, adding 1 Tbsp *(15 ml)* butter to skillet for each batch.

Add the white parts of green onions to skillet. Sauté until tender, about 1 minute. Stir in **White Wine** and boil until liquid is reduced to 2 Tbsp *(30 ml)*, about 3 minutes. Add the cream and simmer until thickened to sauce-like consistency, about 5 minutes. Whisk in Dijon mustard.

Season the sauce to taste with salt and pepper and spoon over the pork. Garnish tenderloin with remaining green onions and serve.

Serves 4

Chicken Balls
in Broth

things you need...

½ lb	*(230 g)*	ground chicken
3 Tbsp	*(45 ml)*	parsley leaves, fresh, minced
1 tsp	*(5 ml)*	Worcestershire sauce
½ tsp	*(2 ml)*	salt
		freshly ground pepper to taste
⅛ tsp	*(.5 ml)*	sage, dried, crumbled
⅓ cup	*(80 ml)*	scallion, white part, thinly sliced
⅓ cup	*(80 ml)*	scallion, green part, thinly sliced
1 Tbsp	*(15 ml)*	butter, unsalted
¼ cup	*(60 ml)*	**White Wine, dry**
4 cups	*(1 L)*	chicken broth
½ cup	*(120 ml)*	snow peas, cut into ½" *(1 cm)* pieces

...now get cookin'

In a bowl, combine the chicken, parsley, Worcestershire, salt, pepper and sage. Blend thoroughly with hands and form the mixture into 1" *(2.5 cm)* balls.

In a large saucepan, cook the white part of the scallion in the butter, over moderately-low heat, until it is softened. Add the **White Wine** and simmer until the wine is reduced by half.

Add the broth and bring to a boil. Add the meatballs and snow peas.

Simmer the soup, covered, for 5 minutes, or until the meatballs are cooked through. Stir in the green part of the scallion. Add salt and pepper to taste.

Serves 2

The oldest winery in Sonoma County, Buena Vista, was established in 1857.

Pesto Pasta
and Sun Dried Tomatoes

things you need...

2 Tbsp	*(30 ml)*	olive oil, extra virgin
1		garlic clove, chopped
½ cup	*(120 ml)*	sun-dried tomatoes, oil-packed, drained, chopped
½ cup	*(120 ml)*	**White Wine, dry**
⅓ cup	*(80 ml)*	pesto sauce (purchased)
15 oz	*(430 g)*	cannellini (white kidney beans), canned, rinsed, drained
8 oz	*(230 g)*	gemelli pasta
¼ cup	*(60 ml)*	parmesan cheese, freshly grated
		salt and pepper to taste

...now get cookin'

Heat the oil in heavy saucepan over medium heat. Add the garlic and sauté for 2 minutes. Add the tomatoes, **White Wine** and pesto and simmer over medium heat until reduced slightly, about 5 minutes. Add beans and stir until heated through.

Meanwhile, cook the pasta according to package directions until tender but still firm to bite, stirring occasionally. Drain pasta, reserving 1 cup *(240 ml)* cooking water.

Add the pasta and cheese to the sauce, then toss to coat. Mix in enough reserved pasta water, ¼ cup *(60 ml)* at a time, to moisten. Season with salt and pepper.

Serves 2

Bay Style
Lamb Chops

things you need...

6 x ½ lb	*(230 g)*	lamb loins
2 Tbsp	*(30 ml)*	olive oil
2 tsp	*(10 ml)*	thyme, fresh, finely chopped
1 tsp	*(5 ml)*	rosemary, fresh, finely chopped
1 tsp	*(5 ml)*	garlic, minced
1 Tbsp	*(15 ml)*	butter
½ cup	*(120 ml)*	**White Wine**
1 cup	*(240 ml)*	lamb stock
¼ cup	*(60 ml)*	tomato pureé
2 Tbsp	*(30 ml)*	black olives, chopped
1 Tbsp	*(15 ml)*	anchovies, chopped
		salt and pepper to taste

...now get cookin'

Rub the lamb loins with oil. Season with thyme and rosemary. Allow to marinate for at least 1 hour prior to grilling.

Sauté the garlic with the butter in a fry pan until lightly brown. Add the **White Wine** and reduce to 1 Tbsp *(15 ml)*. Add lamb stock and tomato pureé and reduce to 1 cup *(240 ml)*. Add olives, anchovies, salt and pepper. Set aside.

Grill the lamb loins to your liking.

To serve, place warm sauce on plates with sliced lamb on top.

Serves 6

Wine has so many organic chemical compounds it is considered more complex than blood serum.

Sips & Tips
the Thirsty Traveler

Gin...A Royal Favorite

Churchill drank it. Roosevelt drank it. And the Queen herself apparently takes a wee tipple now and again. Welcome, fellow Thirsty Travelers, to the genteel pleasures of Gin!

England is synonymous with Gin, but despite its British pedigree, Gin was actually invented in 16th century Holland where it was made from juniper berries. In fact, the name "Gin" is an anglicized version of "genever" – the Dutch word for juniper. Gin started becoming a British phenomenon when soldiers, who were stationed in Holland as part of the war against France, started drinking it before battle. That's where Gin got the nickname "Dutch Courage". Well, as they say, the rest is history!

To make a great Gin, you start with a very high-quality neutral-grain alcohol, usually made from corn or wheat. Then, depending on the style of Gin, a number of especially-selected botanicals are added to the spirit which is distilled once again. Botanicals can be any number of fruits and herbs such as orange or lemon peel, coriander, cardamom pods, orris root or angelica root. While some Gins use up to 20 different botanicals, all must contain juniper berries to legally be called Gin.

There are three basic styles of Gin. The oldest is Geneva, distilled in Holland and matured to give a heavy flavor base. Next up are London Dry Gins, the world's most popular. These are lighter in flavor than Geneva and are great for martinis. Then there's Plymouth Gin. This is the only Gin in the world with a geographic designation (kind of like the Appellation Controlée of French wines) and can only be made in Plymouth, a port city in the deep southwest of England. Plymouth Gin has a more fragrant nose and is weightier than London Dry Gins.

It's Plymouth Gin's fragrancy that makes it an ideal addition to any kitchen. If you have a sweet tooth, try it as an additive in carrot marmalade – an excellent accompaniment to wild fowl or poultry. Gin also helps take gravies or sauces to a bold new level. Is there anyone who doesn't instantly think 'Martini' when they hear the word Gin?

Who knew Gin had so many uses?

Gin distillery in Plymouth, England. ▶

Mayflower
Mussels

things you need...

30		mussels, fresh or frozen
2 Tbsp	*(30 ml)*	olive oil
1		onion, large, chopped
3		garlic cloves, peeled, coarsely chopped
½ cup	*(120 ml)*	parsley leaves, fresh, finely chopped
10 oz	*(295 g)*	tomatoes, canned, peeled, coarsely chopped
4 oz	*(100 g)*	tomato paste
		salt and pepper to taste
1 tsp	*(5 ml)*	white sugar
⅔ cup	*(160 ml)*	**Gin**
2 Tbsp	*(30 ml)*	lemon juice, freshly squeezed

...now get cookin'

If the mussels are fresh, they must be cleaned. If frozen, defrosted.

In a large saucepan, heat the oil and sauté the onions until soft, then add the garlic and parsley.

Sauté for about two minutes, stirring constantly.

Add the chopped tomato, tomato paste, mussels, salt, pepper, sugar and **Gin** and reduce the heat to a simmer.

Add the mussels, until they start opening, then add the lemon juice.

Remove the lid to allow the strong fumes to escape.

Serve on its own, or with plain white rice and or crunchy fresh bread or rolls.

Serves 4   ***(facing page)***

In the late 1580s, a juniper flavored spirit was drunk by British troops who were in Holland fighting in the Dutch War of Independence. The juniper flavored alcohol became known as "Dutch Courage."

Ginned
Cabbage

things you need...

1 lb	*(450 g)*	cabbage, cut lengthwise in 6 wedges leaving the core intact
2		shallots, minced
6		juniper berries
1 tsp	*(5 ml)*	savory, dried
¼ cup	*(60 ml)*	butter
⅓ cup	*(80 ml)*	**Gin**
		salt and pepper to taste

...now get cookin'

In a steamer set over simmering water, steam the cabbage in one layer, covered, for 7 to 10 minutes or until it is tender.

In a large skillet, cook the shallots, the juniper berries and savory in the butter over moderately-low heat, stirring, for 10 minutes.

Add the **Gin** and salt and pepper and simmer the mixture for 1 minute.

Add the cabbage wedges cut side down and cook them, turning them once carefully, for 6 minutes.

Transfer the cabbage with a slotted spatula to a heated serving dish and pour the pan juices over it.

Serves 6

The Thirsty Traveler awaits his skillfully poured dry Gin Martini.

It is law in the United Kingdom that the base alcohol for Gin must be distilled on separate premises from the Gin distillery.

Linguini
Martini

things you need...

¼ **cup**	*(60 ml)*	vegetable oil
4		chicken breasts, skinless, boneless, cut into ½" *(1 cm)* strips
¼ **cup**	*(60 ml)*	flour
¼ **cup**	*(60 ml)*	**Gin**
½ **oz**	*(15 g)*	**Vermouth**
½ **cup**	*(125 ml)*	olives, stuffed, sliced
1¼ **cups**	*(300 ml)*	chicken broth, canned, undiluted
		salt and pepper to taste
12 oz	*(375 g)*	linguini, cooked as per package directions

...now get cookin'

In a skillet, heat the oil over medium heat.

Dust the chicken with flour and place in the saucepan. Brown the chicken on both sides.

Warm the **Gin** in a small container over hot (not boiling) water.

Place a large metal cooking spoon in center of the skillet. Pour in the warm **Gin**. Ignite it with a long match. Slowly stir until flame is extinguished.

Add **Vermouth**, olives, chicken broth, and salt and pepper.

Simmer for 15 minutes, stirring occasionally.

Toss linguini with sauce and serve.

Serves 4

Tom Turkey
Stuffing

things you need...

¾ **cup**	*(175 ml)*	apricots, dried
½ **cup**	*(120 ml)*	**Gin**
4 cups	*(1 L)*	breadcrumbs, dried, fine
½ **cup**	*(120 ml)*	onion, finely chopped
1 Tbsp	*(15 ml)*	sage, dried
1		egg, beaten
1 cup	*(240 ml)*	boiling water
		salt and pepper to taste

...now get cookin'

Place the apricots in a bowl and soak them in the **Gin** for at least 24 hours.

Combine the breadcrumbs, onion and sage together then beat in the egg.

Add the boiling water to soften the crumb mixture, then add the apricots, along with salt and pepper to taste.

Stuff the dressing in the turkey's main cavity and under the skin.

This makes enough dressing for a 12 to 15 lb *(5.5 to 6.75 kg)* turkey.

The Gin and tonic was created as a pleasurable way for Englishmen in tropical colonies to take their daily dose of the bitter tasting malaria fighter, quinine.

Bathtub
Chicken

things you need...

¼ **cup**	*(60 ml)*	lemon juice, freshly squeezed
1 tsp	*(5 ml)*	basil, flakes
1		red onion, chopped
2		garlic cloves, crushed
1 cup	*(240 ml)*	**Gin**
1 cup	*(240 ml)*	water
		salt and pepper to taste
6		chicken breasts, skinless, boneless

...now get cookin'

Combine all ingredients in a bowl and allow to sit for 30 minutes, no longer!

Meanwhile, heat up your grill.

Grill the chicken over medium heat until just done.

In a skillet, sauté the remaining marinade until the juice gels. Pour over chicken and serve.

Serves 6

Plymouth
Salad

things you need...

1		lettuce, butter leaf, medium head
½ **cup**	*(120 ml)*	**Gin**
¼ **cup**	*(60 ml)*	**Vermouth, dry**
¼ **cup**	*(60 ml)*	white vinegar
1		envelope of Mediterranean dressing
⅔ **cup**	*(155 ml)*	olive oil
2		tomatoes, sliced
10		green olives, sliced
		parsley, fresh for garnish

...now get cookin'

Rinse the lettuce leaves and dry completely. Break leaves up and place in a bowl.

Pour the **Gin** over the lettuce and toss so the lettuce gets the taste of **Gin**. Seal the bowl and store in the fridge for up to two days.

When ready to serve, mix up the remaining ingredients in a jar or sealed bottle. Shake well.

Pour dressing over the Gin lettuce, tomatoes and olives. Garnish with parsley.

Serves 4 to 6 **(facing page)**

Sips & Tips
the Thirsty Traveler

Winston Churchill was of the opinion that to make a good dry Martini one needed only to pass a cork from a Vermouth bottle over a glass of Gin.

Bluefish
Fillets in Gin

things you need...

4 x 6 oz	*(170 g)*	bluefish fillets (or cod), skinned
¼ cup	*(60 ml)*	butter, melted
¼ cup	*(60 ml)*	lime juice, freshly squeezed
¼ cup	*(60 ml)*	chives or scallions, minced
¼ cup	*(60 ml)*	**Gin**
¼ cup	*(60 ml)*	breadcrumbs, buttered

...now get cookin'

Marinate the fish for 30 minutes in a mixture of half the butter, all of the lime juice, chives or scallions.

Pat the fillets dry (reserve the marinade) and sauté in a skillet in the remaining butter, cooking about 4 minutes per side.

When almost done, add the marinade and the **Gin**. Heat through and allow the **Gin** to catch fire. After the flame dies down, baste once or twice with the pan juices and cook until done.

Top with buttered breadcrumbs.

Serves 4

Ol' English
Berry Brulée

things you need...

1 cup	*(240 ml)*	berry mixture (i.e. blueberries, raspberries, blackberries)
2 Tbsp	*(30 ml)*	**Gin**
2 Tbsp	*(30 ml)*	icing sugar
12 oz	*(355 ml)*	mascarpone
2 Tbsp	*(30 ml)*	brown sugar
4		dessert biscuits

...now get cookin'

Preheat oven to 400°F *(205° C)*.

Toss the berries, **Gin** and icing sugar together and pile into 4 x ¾ cup *(175 ml)* ramekins. Set aside for 1 hour.

Spoon the mascarpone over the fruit and then sprinkle with brown sugar.

Place in oven until the sugar has begun to brown and the mascarpone is slightly melted.

Serve with crisp dessert biscuits.

Serves 4

Plymouth Gin is the only Gin in the world that has a geographic designation. This means it must be made in the city of Plymouth, in England's far southwest.

Ye Olde
Pumpkin and Gin Pie

things you need...

1		pumpkin, large, to make 1 lb *(500 g)* of pumpkin pureé
1 Tbsp	*(15 ml)*	vegetable oil
1¼ cups	*(300 ml)*	whipping cream
1 x 9"	*(23 cm)*	pie shell, frozen
2		eggs, beaten
¼ cup	*(60 ml)*	brown sugar
1 tsp	*(5 ml)*	cinnamon
¼ tsp	*(1 ml)*	nutmeg, freshly grated

Sauce

1¼ cups	*(300 ml)*	whipping cream
1 tsp	*(5 ml)*	ginger, freshly grated
2 Tbsp	*(30 ml)*	**Gin**
		icing sugar

Behold the beautiful "Raspberry Collins".

...now get cookin'

Preheat oven to 450°F *(230° C)*.

Note: You will need to raise the heat to 450°F *(230° C)* for the pie.

For the pumpkin pureé, chop the pumpkin into large pieces. Drizzle oil on the bottom of a roasting pan to prevent the skins from sticking. Place the pumpkin in the pan skin side down and cover with tin foil. Roast in the oven for 30 to 40 minutes. When soft and golden brown, remove from the oven and cool.

Scrape off the flesh from the skin and remove the seeds. Place pumpkin flesh in a blender and pureé.

In a large mixing bowl, blend the cream, eggs, sugar, cinnamon and nutmeg. Fold in the pumpkin pureé. Pour into pie shell.

Bake at 450°F *(230°C)* for about 15 minutes then lower the heat to 350°F *(180°C)* for about 20 minutes until firm and golden brown.

For the sauce, beat the cream and add the grated ginger. When stiff, add the **Gin** and carefully stir through.

Once the pie has cooled, dust with icing sugar and serve with ginger cream sauce.

Serves 6

In the old days, British sailors were given limes and Gin to ward off scurvy.

Sips & Tips
the Thirsty Traveler

Belgium is Beer Paradise

Mmmm... Beer! When it comes to variety, Belgium is the undisputed Beer capital of the world. Perhaps nowhere else on Earth is this hoppy beverage enjoyed in such variety or held so close to the soul of a people.

Belgium's love affair with Beer can be traced back to the Middle Ages when Trappist monks learned to perfect the art of brewing. Beer's popularity took a definite upswing during the dreaded era of the Plague when a guy named Arnold prescribed it as a healthy replacement for the tainted water that was poisoning people. For his noble efforts, ordinary Arnold became Saint Arnold, patron saint of Beer. Now that's my kind of saint!

Amazing as it seems, there are over 800 Beers made in this country alone. And seeing as how each one is always served in its own glass, Belgium is definitely a place where a Beer drinker could get lost for a long, long time.

Some claim that Belgian Beers are like a meal in themselves. Consider the hearty Trappist Beers, weighing in at a potent seven to 11% alcohol. Then there are Belgium's famed dessert Beers. Sweeter and lighter, these Beers are infused with a wide variety of fruity ingredients, from strawberry or raspberry to cherry and peach. Delightful, delicious, decadent!

Of course, with such an amazing range of palate-pleasing flavors and personalities, Beer has become an integral part of Belgian cuisine. Whether it's scrumptious pork tenderloin served with a rich Beer gravy or strings of sausages stewed in Ale, the people of Belgium eat and drink well at every meal.

Some folks consider Belgium to be Beer heaven. And a visit to the town of Beersell supports that theory. See, Beersell is situated along the Zenne River Valley where it's said the winds carry a special magic – wild yeast. Here, over 100 varieties of wild yeasts float on the breezes, eventually settling into vats of waiting brew. The resulting lambic Beers are famous around the world for their one-of-a-kind tastes and textures. Truly, these are Beers of divine intervention.

So choose your Ale, select the proper glass and raise it in toast to Saint Arnold and the delightful Beers of Belgium.

Beer is a spiritual libation at the Orval ▶ Monastary in the Ardennes in Belgium.

Belgian Beer
Cheese Dip

things you need...

16 oz	*(450 g)*	cream cheese, softened
1 cup	*(240 g)*	cheddar cheese, shredded
½ tsp	*(2 ml)*	garlic powder
½ cup	*(120 ml)*	**Beer**
1		loaf, round bread

...now get cookin'

Place cream cheese, cheddar , garlic and **Beer** in a large bowl. Using an electric mixer, blend until smooth.

Cut the top of round bread out, to make a lid for the bread bowl.

Hollow out the loaf, reserving removed bread pieces. You can cut inside bread into cubes or simply tear pieces out.

Place bread bowl on a platter and cubed pieces for dipping circling the bowl.

Spoon dip into the hollowed bread bowl. Replace bread lid and serve.

Serves 6

Too many Beers to choose from in Brussels, Beer capital of the world!

Escargots
in Amber Ale

things you need...

2		onions, medium, chopped
3		carrots, chopped
2		celery stalks, chopped
¼ cup	*(60 ml)*	parsley stems, chopped
1		turnip, chopped
1		bay leaf
½ tsp	*(2 ml)*	thyme
1 Tbsp	*(15 ml)*	butter
4 cups	*(1 L)*	chicken broth
2 cups	*(480 ml)*	**Amber Ale**
		salt and pepper to taste
36		escargots (6 per person)
6		rosemary sprigs, fresh
		pepper to taste

...now get cookin'

In a large pot of water, steam together onions, carrots, celery, parsley and turnip.

Add 1 Tbsp *(15 ml)* of butter, bay leaf and thyme to the water. Cover and let simmer for 10 to 15 minutes, stirring occasionally.

In a casserole dish, combine the vegetable mixture with the chicken broth, add the **Amber Ale**, salt and pepper.

Let simmer for 4 minutes, add escargots, bring mix to a boil for 1 minute, remove from heat.

Arrange escargots on individual plates, add vegetables and juice. At the last minute, add pepper and place a sprig of rosemary as garnish on each plate.

Serves 6

Sips & Tips

the Thirsty Traveler

There are six Trappist breweries in the world, all of them in Belgium.

Crisp Buttery
Beer Baguettes

Lager
Mustard

things you need...

½ cup	(120 ml)	butter
1 cup	(240 ml)	**Wheat Beer**
1 cup	(240 ml)	parmesan cheese, freshly grated
1		egg
2 Tbsp	(30 ml)	parsley, roughly chopped
4		garlic cloves, roasted
		salt and pepper to taste
16		baguette bread slices

...now get cookin'

Preheat the oven to 325°F (160°C).

Brown the butter in a 9" (23 cm) heavy skillet over medium heat. Remove from heat when the butter starts to foam and turn light brown. Set aside to cool.

Strain through a fine-mesh sieve when cool but still liquid, to remove browned bits of milk proteins.

Place the strained butter, **Wheat Beer**, parmesan cheese, egg, parsley, roasted garlic, and salt and pepper in a food processor fitted with a metal blade. Process on high speed for several minutes or until the mixture is smooth and emulsified. Scrape into a container fitted with a tight lid. Seal and chill until the mixture is solid.

Spread rounds of baguettes on a baking sheet, pour the chilled butter-cheese mixture over and place in oven until golden brown and bubbly.

Serve with soups, salads, dips or deli meats.

Makes 16

things you need...

¼ cup	(60 ml)	brown sugar
1 cup	(240 ml)	**Lager Beer**
2 Tbsp	(30 ml)	brown mustard seeds
2 Tbsp	(30 ml)	yellow mustard powder
½ cup	(120 ml)	cider vinegar
2		shallots, minced
1 tsp	(5 ml)	salt
¼ tsp	(1 ml)	white pepper
2		egg yolks
2 Tbsp	(30 ml)	butter, melted

...now get cookin'

Blend all ingredients in food processor, then place in heavy pan over low heat. Cook until thick and creamy, about 10 minutes, whisking often with wire whisk to prevent curdling.

Let cool to room temperature before chilling. Serve as a condiment for all kinds of meats and deli sandwiches. Keeps up to 2 weeks in a tightly-sealed container in the fridge.

Makes 3½ cups (830 ml)

Be warned when drinking a Trappist Beer. They tend to be very strong, between seven and 11% alcohol.

Sips & Tips

the Thirsty Traveler

Sweet Ale
Pork Fillets

things you need...

4 lbs	*(2 kg)*	pork fillets
½ cup	*(120 ml)*	peanuts, crushed
¼ cup	*(60 ml)*	hazelnuts, crushed
½ cup	*(120 ml)*	parsley, chopped
½ cup	*(120 ml)*	mixed dried fruit, finely chopped
½ cup	*(120 ml)*	olive oil
½ cup	*(120 ml)*	**White Wine**
1 cup	*(240 ml)*	**Ale, dark and sweet**
1 Tbsp	*(15 ml)*	butter

...now get cookin'

Preheat oven to 400°F *(205°C)*.

Place pork fillets in frying pan and brown on each side. Remove from heat and let cool.

Combine the peanuts, hazelnuts, parsley, dried fruit and olive oil in a mixing bowl. Stir until ingredients are mixed together and coated with oil.

Coat the browned pork fillets with the nut and fruit mixture. Then place in an oven safe pan and put in the oven. Bake for 10 minutes.

Remove pork fillets from pan and place on a warmed plate.

Pour the pan juices into a saucepan and add **White Wine** and **Dark Ale**, bring mixture to boil.

Reduce heat and add butter, stirring until melted. Pour hot mixture over each fillet on individual plates.

Serve with seasonal vegetables and potatoes.

Serves 6

Brewed
Eggplant Penne

things you need...

½ cup	*(120 ml)*	olive oil
1		eggplant, medium, peeled, diced
		salt and pepper to taste
1 cup	*(240 ml)*	smoked ham, cubed
1 cup	*(240 ml)*	**Lager Beer**
1 tsp	*(5 ml)*	rosemary, fresh, chopped or ½ tsp dried
1 cup	*(240 ml)*	peas, fresh or frozen
1 lb	*(450 g)*	penne pasta, cooked
		parmesan cheese, freshly grated or shaved
		rosemary sprig, fresh to garnish

...now get cookin'

In a large skillet, heat the olive oil over medium heat.

Put in the eggplant, and season with salt and pepper. Cook, stirring, for about 10 minutes, until it becomes soft.

Stir in the ham, and fry for 2 minutes.

Add the **Beer** and rosemary and bring to a boil until the liquid is reduced by half.

Put in the peas and simmer covered for 2 minutes.

Stir the cooked pasta into the sauce, and cook for 30 seconds to heat through.

Transfer to a serving bowl, sprinkle with plenty of parmesan cheese. Add rosemary sprig and serve.

Serves 4 to 6   ***(facing page)***

Most Belgian pubs carry 300 different Beers, each of which has its own special glass.

Bock
Mushroom Steak

The historic and beautiful Town Square in Leuven, Belgium.

things you need...

¼ cup	(60 ml)	**Bock Beer**
⅓ cup	(80 ml)	olive oil
5		garlic cloves, roasted
3 lbs	(1.5 kg)	flank steak
1 Tbsp	(15 ml)	olive oil
½ cup ea	(120 ml)	oyster, portobello and shiitake mushrooms, thinly sliced
2 Tbsp	(30 ml)	onion, finely minced
		salt and pepper to taste
¾ cup	(180 ml)	**Bock Beer**
1 tsp	(5 ml)	thyme, dried
		hot pepper sauce

...now get cookin'

Blend the **Beer**, the oil and garlic in a blender. Place in a large zip-seal bag with the flank steak, and refrigerate to marinate.

Rub a heavy, nonstick 10" *(25 cm)* saucepan with the 1 Tbsp *(15 ml)* of olive oil. Place over very low heat and gently sauté the mushrooms, sprinkling with onion and a bit of salt. Stir constantly to prevent sticking, and sauté until the mushrooms are almost dehydrated and crisp.

Stir in the ¾ cup *(180 ml)* of **Bock Beer** and the thyme and let simmer. The mushrooms will absorb the beer and return to tenderness.

While the sauce simmers, pan sear the marinated steak in a heavy skillet over high heat to desired doneness. Let the steak rest before carving, slice thin across the grain.

Season the mushroom sauce with salt, pepper and hot pepper sauce and serve a spoonful over each thinly sliced portion of steak.

Serves 6

Corned Beef
and Cabbage in Ale

things you need...

3 lbs	*(1.5 kg)*	corned beef
48 oz	*(1.5 L)*	**Ale**
2		carrots, chopped
12		red potatoes, small
4		onions, quartered
1 tsp	*(5 ml)*	dry mustard
1		thyme, large sprig
1		head cabbage, quartered

...now get cookin'

Place the beef in a large pot with the **Ale**, carrots, potatoes, onions, mustard and thyme. Add just enough cold water to cover.

Bring to a boil and simmer gently 1½ to 2 hours.

Halfway through, check the vegetables. When they are tender, remove them and set aside.

Add the cabbage and cook until tender, about 15 to 30 minutes.

When the meat is tender, return all vegetables to the pot and reheat.

Serve the meat in slices, surrounded by the vegetables and broth.

Serves 4

Namur, Belgium is a haven for Beer lovers including the Thirsty Traveler.

The perfect head of Beer should be no higher than the width of two fingers.

Cheesy Beer Soup

things you need...

¾ cup	(180 ml)	butter
½ cup	(120 ml)	celery, diced
½ cup	(120 ml)	carrots, diced
½ cup	(120 ml)	onion, diced
¾ cup	(180 ml)	flour, all purpose
½ tsp	(2 ml)	dry mustard, ground
14 oz	(430 ml)	chicken broth, can
1 cup	(240 ml)	cheddar cheese, shredded
1 cup	(240 ml)	Monterey Jack cheese, shredded
½ cup	(120 ml)	parmesan cheese, grated
12 oz	(360 ml)	**Amber Ale**
		salt and pepper to taste

...now get cookin'

In a large saucepan over medium-high heat, melt butter. Cook celery, carrots and onion in butter until onion is translucent.

Stir in flour and mustard to coat vegetables.

Pour in broth and simmer until slightly thickened.

Pour mixture into a blender. Pureé mixture and then return it to the saucepan.

When pureéd mixture is hot, begin to stir in cheddar, Monterey Jack and parmesan, a little at a time, alternately with the **Beer**, until all is fully incorporated and melted. Season with salt and freshly ground pepper and serve hot.

Serves 8

Lamb with Sour Cream and Capers

things you need...

2		lamb chops
2 Tbsp	(30 ml)	cooking oil
¾ tsp	(4 ml)	salt
½ cup	(120 ml)	**Lager Beer, dark**
1		bay leaf
1		parsley, sprig
1		thyme, sprig
½ cup	(120 ml)	sour cream
2 Tbsp	(30 ml)	capers

...now get cookin'

Preheat oven to 325°F *(160°C)*.

In a heavy skillet, brown lamb chops well in oil over moderate heat.

Pour off drippings and add remaining ingredients. Cover and simmer about 1½ hours, turning once or twice, until tender. Or cover and bake about 1½ hours.

Place chops on a deep platter. Skim fat from broth, mix in sour cream and capers. Spoon a little sauce over chops and serve.

Serves 2 **(facing page)**

Before thermometers were invented, brewers would dip their thumb into the mash to determine the right temperature to add the yeast. From this we get the phrase, "Rule of Thumb."

The Sparkle of France

Mon dieu! Life is better with bubbly! Is there any drink in the world more associated with love, romance, celebration and pleasure? The Thirsty Traveler says, "I think not."

In hedonistic France, people have been making Wine in the Champagne region for well over a thousand years. Curiously, though, no one figured out how to keep the bubbles in the bottle until the mid 17th century. Legend has it the solution was found at the Abbey d'Hautvillers- home of the legendary monk, Dom Pérignon. That's not quite true. The British get credit for that. But there's no denying Dom Pérignon was the first person to discover the perfect blend of grapes to make top-quality fine Champagne.

See, Dom Pérignon was a blind Benedictine monk who ran the Wine cellars at the Abbey. After years of experimenting with Winemaking techniques and blending grapes, he finally arrived at the right combination for sparkling Wine. And thus the legend of Dom Pérignon was born.

At the first tasting of his new blend, it is said that Pérignon cried out to his fellow monks, "Come quickly, I am drinking stars!"

Remember, that when tasting fine Champagne "stars," you must use your senses! First, pour the Champagne so that the glass is only half full. Examine the color. Admire the different Champagne shades of gold or pink. And watch the bubbles dance.

And now, your nose! The aroma in Champagne can be divided into five categories that evoke flowers, fruits, vegetables, dried fruit or indulgent delicacies like hot rolls, vanilla and spices.

Finally, taste the Wine. Keep it in your mouth for a few seconds. You will not only find the aroma you have identified with your nose, but you will also uncover the true nature of your Champagne – smooth or full-bodied, delicate or complex.

Of course, the above characteristics lend an edge of culinary sophistication to many dishes. After all, what could be better than French cooking combined with French Champagne? From paté to pain du chocolat – Champagne will add a certain sparkle to any meal.

So, here's to good taste and good health. Et voila! Vive la France et vive le Champagne.

Champagne
Vinaigrette

things you need...

1 cup	*(240 ml)*	olive oil
¼ cup	*(60 ml)*	champagne vinegar or white wine vinegar
½ cup	*(120 ml)*	**Champagne**
		salt and pepper to taste
		pinch of sugar

...now get cookin'

Whisk the oil, vinegar and **Champagne** together.

Season to taste with salt and freshly ground pepper. Add the sugar if needed to round out the flavor.

This is great for a romaine lettuce salad with sliced strawberries, mango, mandarin orange and kiwi.

Makes 1½ cups *(360 ml)*, enough for 6 to 8 salads.

Dill Carrots
a la Champagne

things you need...

2 Tbsp	*(30 ml)*	butter
1 lb	*(450 g)*	carrots, thinly sliced
¼ cup	*(60 ml)*	beef stock
½ cup	*(120 ml)*	**Champagne**
1 Tbsp	*(15 ml)*	lemon juice, fresh
1 tsp	*(5 ml)*	dill weed, dried

...now get cookin'

Melt the butter in a heavy saucepan and sauté the carrots for a few minutes over medium heat until they begin to brown.

Add the beef stock and **Champagne** and cover.

Cook carrots until barely tender but still firm.

Remove cover and place on high heat until the liquid is almost cooked away.

Add lemon juice and dill weed and serve.

Serves 4

Press house at Pommery Champagne winery, south of Reims.

Champagne is a sparkling blend of red and white grapes, usually a mixture of Pinot Noir, Pinot Meunier and Chardonnay.

Bubbly
Soup

things you need...

3 cups	(710 ml)	green peas, shelled
1		carrot, medium, sliced
1		onion, medium, sliced
1 oz	(30 g)	salt pork
1		bay leaf
⅛ tsp ea	(.6 ml)	sage, chervil, thyme
3 cups	(710 ml)	chicken stock
½ cup	(120 ml)	**Sherry, dry**
1 tsp	(5 ml)	lemon juice, fresh
		salt and pepper to taste
1 cup	(240 ml)	whipping cream
1 cup	(240 ml)	**Champagne**, room temperature

...now get cookin'

In a saucepan, combine the peas, carrot, onion, salt pork and herbs. Add water to cover. Put lid on and simmer until the peas are very soft.

Remove and discard the carrot, onion, bay leaf and salt pork.

Pureé the soup in a blender. Return the soup to the saucepan and stir in the chicken stock, **Sherry** and lemon juice.

Add salt and pepper and bring the mixture to a boil.

Whip the cream until it holds stiff peaks. Carefully fold the cream into the soup.

Remove from the heat and add the **Champagne**. Serve immediately in heated bowls.

Serves 6

It is law in France that grapes used in the making of Champagne are hand picked. The tractor is there to collect the baskets of grapes.

Surprisingly, much of the finest Champagne comes from black-skinned grapes. The Pinot Noir and Pinot Meunier are made from these colorless-flesh grapes.

Champion Risotto
with Scallops

things you need...

4 Tbsp	*(60 ml)*	butter
¼ cup	*(60 ml)*	green onions, chopped
⅔ cup	*(160 ml)*	arborio rice or white rice, uncooked
1 cup	*(240 ml)*	**Champagne, dry**
1 cup	*(240 ml)*	mushrooms, sliced
2 cups	*(480 ml)*	chicken broth, low salt
¼ tsp	*(1 ml)*	saffron
½ lb	*(230 g)*	scallops, bay or sea
¼ cup	*(60 ml)*	parmesan cheese, freshly grated

...now get cookin'

Melt 2 Tbsp *(30 ml)* of butter in heavy medium saucepan over medium heat. Add onions, sauté 1 minute.

Add rice and sauté for another 2 minutes.

Add **Champagne** and simmer until almost all liquid evaporates, stirring often, about 2 minutes.

Sauté the mushrooms.

Add chicken broth and saffron and simmer until rice is almost tender, stirring often, about 25 minutes. In the last 5 minutes add the parmesan and stir in the sautéed mushrooms.

Grill scallops in the remaining butter until the inside of the scallops are white.

Add three quarters of the scallops to the rice and cook until rice is tender but still firm to bite and mixture is creamy. Add more broth if it's too thick and stir often, about 5 minutes.

Season with salt and pepper. Lay remaining scallops on the risotto to serve.

Serves 2   **(facing page)**

Taking a well deserved rest above a peaceful valley just outside of Paris.

Bottled Champagne is under at least 80 lbs. of pressure per square inch, more than two-and-a-half times the pressure in a car tire.

Sockeye Salmon
Swimming In Champagne

things you need...

6 x 6 oz	*(170 g)*	sockeye salmon fillets
		salt and pepper to taste
1 cup	*(240 ml)*	mushrooms, slivered
1 bottle	*(750 ml)*	**Champagne**
1		onion, medium, sliced
1		parsley and/or thyme, bunch
½ cup	*(120 ml)*	butter, melted

Sauce

3 Tbsp	*(45 ml)*	whipping cream
6		egg yolks
1 cup	*(240 ml)*	butter, melted
		edible flower petals for garnish

...now get cookin'

Remove the skin from the fish, pierce the flesh of the fish with a fork.

Place the fish in a pan, season with salt and pepper, add ½ cup *(120 ml)* of mushroom slivers and just enough **Champagne** to cover the fish. Marinate for 1 hour.

Preheat oven to 350°F *(175°C)*.

Remove fish from marinade and place in a well-buttered, ovenproof pan.

Add onions, thyme, parsley and the rest of the sliced mushrooms, then drizzle with ½ cup *(120 ml)* of melted butter. Bake uncovered. After 20 minutes of cooking time add the marinade the salmon was sitting in.

Bake for another 20 to 30 minutes or until the internal temperature reaches 250° to 255°F *(120° to 125°C)*.

Once cooked, remove the salmon from the liquid and keep it warm on a cooking platter.

To make the sauce, pour the cooking liquid (remaining marinade) into a saucepan, reduce to ¼ cup *(60 ml)*, add cream and reduce until smooth.

Meanwhile, prepare a hollandaise sauce by blending egg yolks and 1 cup *(240 ml)* melted butter. Then carefully fold the hollandaise sauce into the warmed sauce.

Place the sauce on a serving platter and lay the fish on top. Garnish with flower petals.

Serve hot.

Drink any remaining **Champagne** with your meal!

Serves 6 to 8 **(facing page)**

Carbonic gas is created during Champagne's fermentation process, resulting in millions of tiny bubbles. In fact, there are roughly 44 million bubbles in a bottle of sparkling Wine.

BBQ Swordfish
and Champagne Beurre Blanc

things you need...

2 lb	*(1 kg)*	swordfish, center cut
1 Tbsp	*(15 ml)*	olive oil
		salt and pepper to taste
1 cup	*(240 ml)*	**Champagne**
1		lime, freshly squeezed
1 cup	*(240 ml)*	butter, cubed
2 Tbsp	*(30 ml)*	cream

...now get cookin'

Cut swordfish into 6 oz *(170 g)* portions.

Brush the steaks lightly with oil and season with salt and pepper on both sides.

BBQ at medium heat. Cook on first side for 4 minutes, then turn and cook for another 5 minutes.

Place **Champagne** and lime juice in a saucepan and simmer until about ⅓ of the liquid is left.

Remove from heat and add the butter cubes. Stir until the butter is melted.

Add the cream at the end, this will prevent the sauce from breaking.

Place the steaks on a platter or individual plates and pour champagne sauce over.

Serve with your favorite vegetables.

Serves 4

Legend has it that Louis XVI created the Champagne glass. It is said that he used wax moulds formed from Marie Antoinette's breasts.

Creamy
Champagne Chicken

things you need...

1 tsp	*(5 ml)*	garlic, crushed
¼ tsp	*(1 ml)*	salt
4		chicken breasts, boneless, skinless
½ tsp	*(2 ml)*	pepper
1 ⅔ cups	*(400 ml)*	**Champagne**
1 cup	*(240 ml)*	whipping cream

...now get cookin'

Preheat oven to 350°F *(175°C)*.

In a small bowl, mix garlic, salt and pepper.

Rub garlic mixture on chicken breasts and grill on a hot BBQ for 5 to 8 minutes per side, or in the oven for 25 minutes.

Place in ovenproof dish and keep warm.

In a saucepan, heat **Champagne** until reduced by half. Add cream and simmer until thickened, about 30 minutes.

Pour sauce over chicken in oven-proof pan and place in oven for 10 minutes.

Serve with rice and fresh steamed vegetables.

Serves 4

L'Orange
Sorbet

things you need...

¾ cup	*(180 ml)*	sugar
¾ cup	*(180 ml)*	water
1 cup	*(240 ml)*	**Champagne**, chilled
2 Tbsp	*(30 ml)*	orange juice, fresh, strained
¼ tsp	*(1 ml)*	orange-flower water (available at specialty food shops)
1		egg white

...now get cookin'

In a small saucepan, combine the sugar and water, bring the mixture to a simmer over moderate heat, stirring until the sugar is dissolved, then simmer the syrup for 10 minutes. Let the syrup cool and chill it, covered, for 2 hours, or until it is cold.

In a bowl, stir together 1 cup *(240 ml)* chilled syrup, the **Champagne**, the orange juice, and the orange-flower water and freeze the mixture. As the sorbet begins to freeze, whisk it just to combine. Freeze for another hour or until it is frozen but still soft.

In a bowl, beat the egg white until it is frothy, add it to the sorbet, and freeze the sorbet in the freezer until it is firm.

Makes about 2 cups (480 ml)

A raisin dropped into a glass of Champagne will repeatedly bounce up and down between the top and the bottom of the glass.

Sips & Tips
the Thirsty Traveler

Jamaican Rum 'Mon'

Jah, mon! Come take a reggae splash in Jamaica – island in the sun! Here, there is no shortage of all things pleasurable: surf, sand, music and Rum. Indeed, Rum has played an integral role in Jamaica's history for well over 250 years. Way back in 1749, Jamaica became home to one of the first distilleries to produce this golden elixir. And you know that where there's Rum, there's pirates.

Jamaica provided a haven for notorious buccaneers like Captain Henry Morgan (who later switched sides and became lieutenant governor) as well as "Calico Jack" Rackham and Charles Vane (who later met their deaths at the end of a rope in Jamaica's infamous Gallows Point).

They say that back when the pirate ships roamed the Caribbean, there was one bar for every 10 men. But Rum is more than just a drink to the local people of this island paradise. Today, it is a medicine, a sacrament, a condiment and a libation.

Internationally-renowned as a Caribbean playground, Jamaica offers more to the Thirsty Traveler than sun and Rum. Take Jamaica's famous jerk, for instance. Jerk is a fiery blend of spices, peppers, onions and – to be authentic – a splash of Rum. Throughout the island you can find roadside jerk-stands serving jerk chicken or pork. It's fast food Jamaican-style; delicious, zesty snacks meant to be enjoyed with fresh coconut water and maybe a splash of sweet Jamaican Rum.

So take it from the Thirsty Traveler: get up, stand up and enjoy the best of this sun-splashed island's food and drink.

Cheers, mon, to Jamaican Rum!

Glorious sunset over palm trees in ▶ Ocho Rios, Jamaica.

Rockin' Rum
Bean Soup

things you need...

2 cups	*(480 ml)*	black beans, dried
2 cups	*(480 ml)*	onion, chopped
6		parsley sprigs, chopped
1 cup	*(240 ml)*	celery, chopped
2 Tbsp	*(30 ml)*	thyme, fresh, chopped
1		bay leaf
3 Tbsp	*(45 ml)*	butter, unsalted
1		ham hock, large
6 cups	*(1.5 L)*	beef broth
4 cups	*(1 L)*	water
		salt and pepper to taste
⅓ cup	*(80 ml)*	**Rum, dark**
		lime juice to taste
		parsley, fresh, chopped for garnish
		lemon, sliced for garnish
		sour cream, dollop

...now get cookin'

To clean the beans cover them with cold water. Let them sit for 5 minutes and remove anything that floats. Repeat to be sure all dirt and foreign matter is removed and then drain.

In cold water, submerge the beans and let them soak for 2 to 4 hours. Drain beans through a colander.

In a heavy kettle, cook onion, parsley, celery, thyme, and bay leaf in the butter over medium-low heat, stirring, for 10 minutes.

Add ham hock, beans, broth, water, salt and pepper.

Bring the mixture to a boil, reduce heat and simmer uncovered. Add more water if necessary to keep beans covered.

Simmer for 3 hours.

Remove ham hock and bay leaf.

Put ½ of the mixture through a blender, into a large bowl and then return it to the kettle.

Stir in **Rum**, lime juice, and salt and pepper.

Serve in individual bowls and garnish with parsley, lemon slices and sour cream.

Serves 4   ***(facing page)***

The name Jamaica was derived from the country's Arawak Indian name "Xaymaca", which means, "The Land of Wood and Water".

Spiced
Rum Spread

things you need...

2 to 3		garlic cloves, diced or pressed
1 Tbsp	*(15 ml)*	sugar
1 Tbsp	*(15 ml)*	lemon juice
2 Tbsp	*(30 ml)*	oil
2 Tbsp	*(30 ml)*	**Rum**, **Spiced** or **Aged**
1		onion, small, diced
½		red bell pepper, diced
½		green bell pepper, diced
8 oz	*(230 g)*	cream cheese, softened
		assorted crackers

...now get cookin'

Whisk the garlic, sugar, lemon juice, oil and **Rum** together in a small bowl.

Pour marinade over the onions and peppers, and let sit for 1 hour.

Drain any liquid off the onions and peppers and add the softened cream cheese. Mix into a pasty spread.

Serve with assorted crackers or crisp bread.

Makes 2 cups (480 ml)

Reggae
Rum Ribs

things you need...

4 lbs	*(2 kg)*	spare ribs or country style ribs
1		Scotch Bonnet pepper, remove seeds, stem, veins
½ cup	*(120 ml)*	**Rum, dark**
¼ cup	*(60 ml)*	lime juice, fresh
1 Tbsp	*(15 ml)*	lime zest, grated
¾ cup	*(180 ml)*	peanut oil
¼ cup	*(60 ml)*	cilantro leaves, chopped
3		garlic cloves, minced or pressed
		salt and pepper to taste

...now get cookin'

Preheat oven to 350°F *(175° C)*.

Boil the ribs for 30 to 40 minutes or until tender.

Wrap in a double thickness of aluminum foil and bake in the oven for 1½ hours.

Remove ribs from the oven, unwrap them and drain the drippings, place in a shallow baking dish.

Mix the remaining ingredients in jar or dressing shaker. Shake well to combine.

Pour marinade over the ribs and let sit at room temperature for 1 hour.

Place ribs on a BBQ at low-medium heat for 30 minutes, turning and basting with marinade from the dish.

Alternatively, you can bake the ribs in oven for 30 minutes.

Serve with rice or pasta and fresh vegetables.

Serves 4

Jamaican Scotch Bonnet peppers are one of the world's hottest peppers, about 30-50 times hotter than a jalapeno. Wear gloves when handling these babies and don't touch your face (or other precious parts).

Kingston Chops

things you need...

4		pork chops, center cut, bone in

Marinade

1 cup	(240 ml)	**Rum, Spiced** or **Aged**
¼ cup	(60 ml)	lime juice, freshly squeezed
2 Tbsp	(30 ml)	olive oil
3		garlic cloves, chopped
1		cilantro, bunch, roughly chopped
		salt and pepper to taste

Sauce

1 Tbsp	(15 ml)	olive oil, extra virgin
3		garlic cloves, thinly sliced
3 Tbsp	(45 ml)	lime, orange and/or grape-fruit juice, freshly squeezed
⅛ tsp	(.5 ml)	cumin
		salt and pepper to taste

...now get cookin'

Combine the marinade ingredients together in a glass bowl that can be tightly sealed. Mix well. Add pork chops, seal and shake to cover pork chops.

Place in the fridge and let the chops marinate for 1½ to 2 hours, turning the chops once or twice.

To make the garlic sauce, heat the olive oil in a small frying pan and add the garlic until it is lightly browned.

Add the fruit juices and the cumin (juices will splatter when they touch the oil).

Remove pan from heat and add salt and pepper.

Lightly oil a clean grill with nonstick spray. Preheat to medium and then grill the chops until the meat is no longer pink inside.

Place the chops on a serving plate, pour the garlic sauce over them and serve.

Serves 4

A hot handful of fiery Jamaican peppers.

Bottles of Rum must indicate the country of origin and its proof, which can range from 80 to 151.

Jamaican
Jerk Chicken

things you need...

Jerk seasoning

1		red onion, chopped
1½ tsp	(7 ml)	thyme, dried
1 tsp	(5 ml)	allspice, ground
½ tsp	(2 ml)	cinnamon, ground
4 tsp	(20 ml)	white pepper
¼ cup	(60 ml)	green onion tops, chopped
2 tsp	(10 ml)	salt
¼ tsp	(1 ml)	nutmeg, ground
5		jalapenos, small
2 Tbsp	(30 ml)	olive oil or vegetable oil
		Rum, splash

Chicken

1		whole chicken, halved
1		lime, halved
		pinch of salt
5 Tbsp	(70 ml)	Jerk rub seasoning (from recipe above)

...now get cookin'

Place all the ingredients for the Jerk seasoning into a food processor. Mix on high for 15 pulses.

Makes ⅔ cup *(140 ml)*, which will keep in the fridge for up to 4 months.

With your hands, rub cleaned chicken halves with lime, salt and the Jerk seasoning you've made.

Marinate in the fridge overnight for the best results.

When you're ready to cook, place chicken on BBQ at medium-low heat for 45 minutes.

Let chicken sit for 10 minutes before cutting into quarters.

Serves 4 **(facing page)**

Aged Rum being poured from the keg.

When Jamaicans catch a chill, they apply Rum to their foreheads. To ward off a cold, they drink a mixture of Rum, lime and honey.

Yummy Rummy
Beef Stew

things you need...

3		bacon slices, chopped
2 lbs	(1 kg)	beef, lean, cubed, dredged in flour
1		onion, large, chopped
2		garlic cloves, chopped
1		green bell pepper, small, chopped
2 cups	(480 ml)	beef stock
16 oz	(455 g)	tomatoes, canned, chopped, undrained
⅓ cup	(80 ml)	**Rum, amber**
		Worcestershire sauce, dash
1		bay leaf
½ tsp	(2 ml)	thyme
4		carrots, sliced
2		potatoes, medium, cubed
		salt and pepper to taste

...now get cookin'

In a Dutch oven or heavy cooking pot, cook bacon until crispy. Add the beef in small batches and brown.

Add onions, garlic and pepper and cook until soft.

Add beef stock, tomatoes, **Rum**, Worcestershire sauce, spices and salt and pepper. Stir well, cover and cook over low heat for about 45 minutes.

Add carrots and potatoes and continue cooking for 20 minutes or until vegetables are cooked.

Serves 6

Calico Jack
Sweet Potatoes

things you need...

1 Tbsp	(15 ml)	olive oil
3		sweet potatoes, medium, peeled, sliced
½ cup	(120 ml)	chicken broth
½ cup	(120 ml)	orange juice, freshly squeezed
3 Tbsp	(45 ml)	**Rum, dark**
2 tsp	(10 ml)	cornstarch
⅛ tsp	(.5 ml)	white pepper
⅛ tsp	(.5 ml)	cumin, ground
		salt to taste
2 Tbsp	(30 ml)	parsley, fresh

...now get cookin'

Heat oil in a large frying pan over medium-high heat. Add potato slices and brown lightly on both sides. Add broth, cover and bring to a boil.

Reduce heat and simmer until potatoes are slightly tender (about 10 minutes).

Uncover and continue to cook until the liquid evaporates (about 5 minutes).

In a bowl, mix orange juice, **Rum**, cornstarch, white pepper, cumin and salt. Add this mixture to the pan, bring it to a boil and stir until thickened.

Top with fresh parsley.

Serves 4 to 6

The origin of the word "Rum" is still under debate. One term, "rumbullion" means "stem stew" in Creole, and "an uproar" in British slang. Some believe the Latin name for sugar, "saccharum", may have been shortened to Rum.

Sweet Jamaican
Fondue

things you need...

1½ Tbsp	*(20 ml)*	**Rum, white**
7 oz	*(200 g)*	chocolate, milk or dark
4 tsp	*(20 ml)*	butter
2 Tbsp	*(30 ml)*	yogurt, plain
½ cup	*(120 ml)*	whipping cream
		fruit pieces, sweet bread and marshmallows

...now get cookin'

Place **Rum**, chocolate and butter together in a saucepan on low heat. Cook until melted together.

Remove from heat, and stir in yogurt and cream.

Serve with fruit pieces, sweet bread and marshmallows for dipping.

Serves 4

A cooper assembles a cask that will soon contain premium Rum.

Cabaña
Bananas

things you need...

4		bananas, ripe
4 Tbsp	*(60 ml)*	brown sugar
4 tsp	*(20 ml)*	butter
1 cup	*(240 ml)*	orange juice
1 Tbsp	*(15 ml)*	**Rum, dark**
4 Tbsp	*(60 ml)*	coconut cream or ice cream

...now get cookin'

Preheat oven to 350°F *(175°C)*.

Place bananas in a greased baking dish, sprinkle with sugar and place butter on top in small dollops.

Mix orange juice and **Rum** and pour around the bananas.

Bake for 20 minutes.

Serve with a dollop of coconut cream or ice cream.

Serves 4

In the 1800s, Rum was considered excellent for cleaning hair and keeping it healthy.

Sips & Tips
the Thirsty Traveler

Black Gold, Irish Nectar

The Emerald Isle is a glorious feast for the senses. From its famous authors, playwrights and musicians, to the lore of the leprechaun to the lure of the land, Ireland is a sensual treat in every way. Enhancing the romance, of course, is thick, creamy, tasty Stout.

The Irish love their Stout – basically a dark, rich and bitter beer – and have for centuries. This love affair, though, began as the result of a happy accident across the Irish Sea in London's East End.

While roasting barley malt in preparation to make ale, a local brewer mistakenly burned the batch. Not wanting to lose his shirt or the product, he decided to complete the beer-making process. The resulting brew was near-black, syrupy and quite bitter. But the hard-living porters hauling heavy loads around London's dockside took an immediate and immense liking to it – indeed, such a liking that this early Stout become known as "porter".

Then a chap named Arthur Guinness came along and took the recipe back to Dublin. Well, boyos, the rest is history. Stout soon stood tall as the favored beverage in pubs across the country. Like beautiful County Cork down in the nation's lush southwest corner. Here, Murphy's Brewery and Beamish & Crawford produced their own versions of this Irish favorite, and the Thirsty Traveler is delighted to report they are still going strong today.

Irish cuisine has enjoyed a renaissance over the past decade. Culinary hot spots, like the west coast city of Galway, famous for its annual oyster festival, are making the world take notice. Then there's Kinsale, a lovely seaside town an hour south of Cork. This place is a haven for people who love great food. Kinsale even has an annual Festival of Fine Food where local restaurants really strut their stuff.

There is nothing quite so scrumptious as downing a fresh, rich, fatty oyster and chasing it with a sip of full-bodied Stout. It seems the dry roast of the Stout provides the perfect foil to the oyster's subtle, salty tang. Incredible! For a tasty variation, try oysters soaked in Stout. If you're a beef eater, try seared tenderloin stuffed with Stout-soaked oysters. Yes, it is as decadent as it sounds!

The pint is a way of life in Ireland. While it gives some people the gift of the gab, it also gives the gift of good grub. Stout! Slainte!

Historic St. Patrick's Rock is an imposing site ▶ as it stands in County Tipperary, Ireland.

Limbered Up
Lamb

things you need...

2 lbs	*(1 kg)*	leg of lamb or mutton, boneless
2 cups	*(480 ml)*	**Stout**
2		onions, thinly sliced
½ tsp	*(1 ml)*	malt or cider vinegar
1 tsp	*(5 ml)*	salt
		pepper to taste
2 Tbsp	*(30 ml)*	butter

...now get cookin'

Cut lamb into thin slices across the grain.

Place in a heavy pan and add the **Stout**, onions and vinegar, cover and simmer for an hour.

Add the salt, pepper and butter and continue simmering for 30 minutes, or until tender.

Serves 4

Stout
Mayonnaise

things you need...

½ cup	*(120 ml)*	cream
1 cup	*(240 ml)*	mayonnaise
½ cup	*(120 ml)*	**Stout**

...now put it together...

In a medium bowl mix cream, mayo and **Stout**, in that order. Stir well.

Serve with salad, tiger prawns or shrimp.

Stout Mayo can be kept in the fridge for up to 4 weeks.

Serves 4

Stout Steak
Carpet-Bagger

things you need...

4 x 8 oz	*(250 g)*	beef tenderloin fillets
4 Tbsp	*(60 ml)*	Worcestershire sauce
1 tsp	*(5 ml)*	liquid smoke
1 cup	*(240 ml)*	**Stout**
8		fresh oysters, large
		salt and pepper to taste

...now get cookin'

Preheat oven to 350°F *(175°C)*.

The day before you serve the carpet-bagger, mix the Worcestershire sauce and liquid smoke, placing the beef fillets in the mixture and marinate over night.

In a medium bowl, pour in **Stout**, add oysters and let sit for 1 to 2 hours.

Take your beefsteaks and make a small incision in the side of each.

Insert 2 oysters in the incision, depending on size, and secure with a toothpick.

In an ovenproof skillet, sear steaks on both sides for 2 to 3 minutes on high heat.

Place skillet in oven for 10 minutes or until desired meat liking.

Serve with vegetables of your choice.

Serves 4   ***(facing page)***

Guinness draught was first introduced to the U.S. in 1967.

Stout-Brined
BBQ Pork Chops

Irish Honey
Mustard

things you need...

2 cups	*(480 ml)*	water
2 cups	*(480 ml)*	**Stout**
¼ cup	*(60 ml)*	salt, coarse
3 Tbsp	*(45 ml)*	brown sugar, dark, packed
3 Tbsp	*(45 ml)*	molasses, mild flavored (light)
1 cup	*(240 ml)*	ice cubes
6		pork chops, center cut, bone in, 1¼" *(3.5 cm)* thick
7		garlic cloves, minced
1 Tbsp	*(15 ml)*	black pepper, coarsely ground
2 tsp	*(10 ml)*	salt
2 tsp	*(10 ml)*	sage leaves, dried

things you need...

1 cup	*(240 ml)*	yellow mustard seeds
1 cup	*(240 ml)*	brown mustard seeds
1½ cups	*(360 ml)*	**Stout**
¾ cup	*(180 ml)*	cider vinegar
⅓ cup	*(80 ml)*	dry mustard, powder
1 Tbsp	*(15 ml)*	brown sugar
4 Tbsp	*(60 ml)*	honey
1 tsp	*(5 ml)*	salt
1		onion, small, minced
4		garlic cloves, minced or pressed
1 tsp	*(5 ml)*	allspice
½ tsp	*(2 ml)*	tumeric

...now get cookin'

Combine water, **Stout**, salt, brown sugar and molasses in large bowl. This is your brine.

Stir until salt and sugar dissolve then stir in ice.

Place pork chops in large freezer or zip plastic bag. Pour **Stout** brine over pork chops, seal bag. Refrigerate 4 hours, turning bag occasionally.

Heat BBQ to medium-high. Remove pork chops from Stout brine and pat dry.

Mix garlic, pepper, salt and sage in small bowl.

Rub garlic mixture over both sides of pork chops. Grill chops for about 10 minutes per side, occasionally moving chops to cooler part of rack if burning.

Transfer chops to platter. Cover with foil and let stand 5 minutes before serving.

Serves 6

...now get cookin'

With a mortar and pestle crush the yellow and brown mustard seeds into a fine powder.

In a medium mixing bowl, mix **Stout**, mustard seed powder, vinegar, dry mustard, brown sugar, honey and salt. It should be a little more runny than store bought mustard.

Stir in finely minced onion, garlic, allspice and tumeric.

Great in salad dressings, or try it on your favorite ham or turkey sandwich alongside the Stout mayonnaise! (see recipe on page 74)

Makes 3½ cups (830 ml)

Dark Beer is rich in flavonoids. This substance gives these drinks their color and is also believed to have a positive effect on blood pressure and cholesterol levels.

Peasant
Sirloin Stew

things you need...

½ **lb**	*(230 g)*	boneless beef sirloin, cut into 1" *(2.5 cm)* cubes
		salt and pepper to taste
1 Tbsp	*(15 ml)*	butter
2		carrots, large, peeled, sliced
1 cup	*(240 ml)*	pearl onions
2 tsp	*(10 ml)*	flour, all purpose
⅔ **cup**	*(160 ml)*	beef broth
⅓ **cup**	*(80 ml)*	**Stout** or **Dark Ale**

...now get cookin'

Sprinkle beef with salt and pepper.

Melt butter in a heavy medium skillet over high heat. Add beef and sauté until brown on all sides, about 5 minutes.

Using a slotted spoon, transfer beef to bowl.

Reduce heat to medium-low. Add carrots and onions to skillet, toss to coat with pan juices.

Add flour, stir 1 minute. Add broth and **Stout**.

Add beef and any juices collected in bowl. Cover skillet and simmer until beef and carrots are tender. Stir occasionally, about 15 minutes. Season with salt and pepper.

Serve over rice or boiled potatoes.

Serves 2

Dublin
Sautéed Beets

things you need...

8 lbs	*(3.5 kg)*	beets, including the greens (4 lbs *(2 kg)* without the greens)
3 Tbsp	*(45 ml)*	**Stout** or **Dark Ale**
1 Tbsp	*(15 ml)*	red wine vinegar
¼ **cup**	*(60 ml)*	butter, unsalted
		salt and pepper to taste

...now get cookin'

Trim beets leaving 2" *(5 cm)* of the stem ends intact and reserving 1 lb *(450 g)* of the beet greens.

Discard coarse stems of the reserved beet greens and leaves.

Wash well, spin dry and chop very coarsely.

In a large pot, cover the beets with 2" *(5 cm)* of cold water and bring to a boil. Simmer for 20 to 35 minutes or until they are tender.

Drain the beets and run cold water over them to slip off their skins and stems. Discard skins and stems.

In a skillet, bring to a boil the **Stout** and the vinegar and whisk in 2 Tbsp *(30 ml)* of the butter.

Cut beets into quarters and stir into skillet. Cover and keep the beets warm.

In a large skillet, heat the remaining butter over moderately high heat until the foam subsides. In it sauté the reserved beet greens, stirring, for 5 minutes, or until they are tender.

Stir in salt and pepper. Arrange the greens around the edge of a platter and mound the beets in the center.

Serves 8

About 13 million glasses of Stout are drunk around the world each day.

77

Ginger
Spice Loaf

things you need...

1 cup	*(240 ml)*	**Stout**
1 cup	*(240 ml)*	molasses
½ Tbsp	*(8 ml)*	baking soda
3		eggs
½ cup	*(120 ml)*	sugar
½ cup	*(120 ml)*	brown sugar, firmly packed
¾ cup	*(180 ml)*	vegetable oil
2 cups	*(480 ml)*	flour, all purpose
2 Tbsp	*(30 ml)*	ginger, ground
1½ tsp	*(7 ml)*	baking powder
¾ tsp	*(4 ml)*	cinnamon, ground
¼ tsp	*(1 ml)*	cloves, ground
¼ tsp	*(1 ml)*	nutmeg, freshly grated or powdered
⅛ tsp	*(.5 ml)*	cardamom, ground
1 Tbsp	*(15 ml)*	ginger root, fresh, grated or peeled

...now get cookin'

Preheat oven to 350°F *(175° C)*.

Butter and flour a 9" X 5" *(22 x 12 cm)* loaf pan.

In a large saucepan over high heat, add the **Stout** and molasses, bring to a boil. Turn off heat, add baking soda. Allow to sit until foam dissipates.

In a bowl, whisk eggs and both sugars. Then whisk in the oil.

In a separate bowl, mix flour, ginger, baking powder, cinnamon, cloves, nutmeg and cardamom.

Combine Stout and egg mixtures. Whisk liquid into flour mixture, half at a time. Add the ginger root and stir to combine.

Pour batter into pan and bake 1 hour. Transfer to a wire rack to cool. Serve naked (the cake that is) or top with whipped cream.

Serves 8

Choc-full-o
Stout Pie

things you need...

1½ cups	*(360 ml)*	graham crackers, crushed
⅓ cup	*(80 ml)*	butter, melted
12 oz	*(340 g)*	chocolate, dark
24		marshmallows, large
		pinch of salt
⅔ cup	*(160 ml)*	**Stout**
⅓ cup	*(80 ml)*	evaporated milk
1 tsp	*(5 ml)*	vanilla
1 Tbsp	*(15 ml)*	**Crème de Cacao Liqueur**
1 cup	*(240 ml)*	whipping cream

...now get cookin'

Preheat oven to 350°F *(175°C)*.

In a medium mixing bowl, add melted butter to crushed graham crackers and mix until well blended.

Using fingers, press crust mixture into bottom and up the sides of pie plate.

Bake crust for about 6 minutes until set. (Or use a prepared graham cracker crust.)

Place chocolate, marshmallows and salt in a blender. Blend until well mixed and chocolate is finely ground.

In two separate saucepans (in order to prevent curdling), heat **Stout** in one pan and evaporated milk in the other until very hot, but not boiling.

Pour **Stout** and milk into blender with chocolate marshmallow mixture and blend for one minute.

Add vanilla and **Crème de Cacao** and blend a little more.

Pour into the crust and refrigerate overnight.

Beat the whipping cream until stiff, garnish pie slices and serve.

Serves 8   **(facing page)**

A pint of Stout has fewer calories than a pint of skimmed milk or orange juice.

From Russia with Voda

For more than 600 years, Vodka has been an inalienable part of Russian culture and cuisine. History tells us that the first lucky soul to taste Vodka's bite was likely an 8th Century Arab alchemist living in the area of what we know as modern-day Morocco. Seems this fellow stumbled across a way to ferment ancient grains into a spirit possessing all sorts of perception-altering properties.

Sometime in the mid-1200s, this crude knowledge of Vodka-making migrated north into Europe where wheat, rye and barley were common. Here, Italian alchemists kept their distillation methods top secret — only providing the spirit to physicians, as a remedy for a vast variety of ailments, and to the clergy, who thoroughly integrated this spirit into religious ceremonies of every kind.

Vodka came to Russia in the 14th Century when Italian merchants, looking to exploit new markets, began shipping their Vodka northward. And this is where Vodka likely got its name. See, the Russian word for water is "voda", and this evolved into what we now know as "Vodka".

Contrary to popular belief, true Russian Vodkas are made from wheat, not potatoes. The Russians have been growing wheat for a thousand years but the ubiquitous tuber didn't arrive there until the late 1700s. Polish Vodkas, on the other hand, have almost always been produced from spuds.

One of the most important processes in creating truly Russian Vodka is to filter the newly-distilled spirit through birch charcoal. Birch is synonymous with the remote Russian landscape, and you see it nearly everywhere you go. Filtering through birch charcoal removes nearly 100% of the fused oils and impurities, resulting in a wonderfully clean, smooth spirit.

Here's a beautiful custom involving bread and Vodka. When drinking Vodka, one must first offer a toast to the others at the table. You toss back your Vodka shot (served at room temperature, not cold or frozen!) and then immediately take a slice of black bread and sniff it deeply. The rich aroma of the bread helps to complement the taste of the Vodka while cleansing your nasal passages. Try it!

Spaceba, Russia and Na zdorovje to Russian Vodka!

Looking towards Red Square, at Lenin's Tomb ▶ and the Kremlin clock tower.

Moscow
Marinade

things you need...

¼ **cup**	*(60 ml)*	**Vodka**
⅓ **cup**	*(75 ml)*	lemon juice, fresh
1 **Tbsp**	*(15 ml)*	lemon zest
¼ **cup**	*(60 ml)*	canola oil
¼ **cup**	*(60 ml)*	olive oil, pure or virgin
¼ **cup**	*(60 ml)*	dill, fresh, chopped
¼ **cup**	*(60 ml)*	scallions, white part only, chopped
½ **tsp**	*(2 ml)*	sugar
		salt and pepper to taste

...now get cookin'

In a mixing bowl, combine the **Vodka**, lemon juice and lemon zest.

Whisk in the oils a little at a time. Add the dill, scallions and sugar.

Season to taste with salt and pepper.

This marinade works well with salmon or tuna steaks (marinate for 2 to 4 hours).

Makes about 2 cups *(480 ml)*

Naked
Tomatoes

things you need...

2 **quarts**	*(1.8 L)*	tomatoes, small, firm,
⅓ **cup**	*(80 ml)*	**Vodka, Lemon**
3 **Tbsp**	*(45 ml)*	white wine vinegar
1 **Tbsp**	*(15 ml)*	sugar
2 **Tbsp**	*(30 ml)*	dill leaves, fresh
		salt and pepper to taste
1		lemon, firm

...now get cookin'

Cut a small shallow X at the stem end of each tomato and have a bowl of ice water ready.

In a saucepan of boiling water, blanch the tomatoes, 3 at a time for 2 to 3 seconds and immediately transfer to ice water to stop cooking. (Tomatoes should still be firm but skins should slip off easily)

In a bowl, stir together **Vodka**, vinegar and sugar until sugar is dissolved.

Peel tomatoes and de-seed, then add to Vodka mixture.

Add dill, salt and pepper to the tomatoes, tossing gently.

Marinate the tomatoes, cover and chill for at least 30 minutes and up to 1 hour.

With a citrus zester, cut 2 Tbsp *(30 ml)* zest in strips from the lemon.

Just before serving, gently toss tomatoes with a rubber spatula and sprinkle with zest.

Serve tomatoes with small forks or wooden picks.

*Serves 4   **(facing page)***

Russians first started distilling Vodka over 600 years ago.

Lenin's
Linguine

things you need...

1 cup	*(240 ml)*	water
½ cup	*(120 ml)*	sun-dried tomatoes, sliced
3 cups	*(710 ml)*	water
16		asparagus spears
4 tsp	*(20 ml)*	butter, unsalted
1 lb	*(450 g)*	shrimp, large, peeled, deveined
8 oz	*(250 g)*	linguine
1 cup	*(240 ml)*	shallots, sliced
½ cup	*(120 ml)*	**Vodka**
1 cup	*(240 ml)*	tomato sauce
1 cup	*(240 ml)*	milk, 2%
¼ tsp	*(1 ml)*	salt
½ cup	*(120 ml)*	basil, fresh, thinly sliced

...now get cookin'

Heat the 1 cup *(240 ml)* water until boiling and pour in the sun-dried tomatoes.

Allow to stand for about 15 minutes until the sun-dried tomatoes are soft.

Then drain the liquid into a sauce pan, heat the liquid on high heat until it boils and reduces to ¼ cup *(60 ml)*. Set aside.

Heat the 3 cups *(710 ml)* of water to a shiver in a medium sized skillet.

Add the asparagus and blanch for about 2 to 3 minutes, until they begin to turn bright green.

Remove and let dry on a paper towel. When they are cool, cut them in 2" *(5 cm)* segments.

Melt the butter in a large skillet over medium-high heat.

Add the shrimp and sauté until slightly firm (no more than about 2 minutes on each side). Remove shrimp to a plate.

Cook linguine according to package directions.

While the pasta cooks, add the shallots to the already used skillet and cook over medium heat until they begin to soften and turn slightly brown, about 7 to 10 minutes.

Reduce the heat to low and add the **Vodka**.

Cook briefly and then add the tomato sauce, milk and salt.

After this has cooked for about 3 minutes, add the asparagus and sun-dried tomatoes. Simmer until tomatoes are tender, about 4 minutes.

Add shrimp, toss to coat and allow to cook for another 4 minutes until the shrimp is heated through.

Drain the linguine. Add the pasta to the tomato sauce and toss to coat well.

Season to taste with fresh pepper.

Serve topped with basil.

Serves 4

A rustic Russian cottage, or dacha, on the outskirts of Kirov.

Ian Fleming's super spy James Bond, popularized Vodka in the 1960s when he asked for a Vodka Martini to be "shaken not stirred."

Rasputin's
Rigatoni

things you need...

7 oz	(200 g)	jar of roasted red peppers
¼ lb	(125 g)	prosciutto, chopped
2 cups	(480 ml)	whipping cream
28 oz	(800 g)	tomatoes, canned, crushed
2 Tbsp	(30 ml)	**Vodka**
2 Tbsp	(30 ml)	parsley, fresh, chopped
2 tsp	(10 ml)	garlic powder
1½ tsp	(7 ml)	white sugar
1 tsp	(5 ml)	salt
¼ tsp	(1 ml)	black pepper, ground
⅛ tsp	(0.5 ml)	red pepper flakes, crushed (optional)
1 cup	(240 ml)	parmesan cheese, grated
1 lb	(450 g)	rigatoni pasta

...now get cookin'

Drain roasted peppers, reserving a small amount of the liquid. Cut peppers into strips.

Combine prosciutto, cream, tomatoes, **Vodka**, peppers with reserved liquid, parsley, garlic powder, sugar, salt, pepper and red pepper flakes in a saucepan. Cover.

Cook over medium heat, stirring often, until the sauce comes to a boil.

Reduce heat, and simmer for 30 minutes.

Meanwhile, cook pasta according to package directions. Drain, and transfer to a large serving bowl.

Stir cheese into the sauce and pour sauce over rigatoni.

Serves 8

Comrades'
Chicken Pasta

things you need...

1 lb	(450 g)	penne pasta
2 cups	(480 ml)	marinara sauce
16 oz	(450 g)	tomatoes, canned, diced, with roasted garlic juice
⅓ cup	(80 ml)	basil, fresh, chopped
¼ cup	(60 ml)	**Vodka**
¾ tsp	(4 ml)	red pepper, dried, crushed
1		chicken, whole roasted, skinned, meat shredded into bite-size strips
		salt and pepper to taste
¼ cup	(60 ml)	parmesan cheese, freshly grated

...now get cookin'

Cook pasta according to package directions. Cook until tender but still firm. Drain. Return to pot.

Meanwhile, in a large saucepan, heat the marinara sauce with the tomatoes and juices, basil, **Vodka**, and crushed red pepper over medium heat until hot, about 5 minutes.

Add shredded chicken and stir until heated through.

Add sauce to pasta and toss.

Season with salt and pepper.

Transfer to serving bowl. Sprinkle with parmesan cheese and serve.

Serves 4

There is a Russian ritual of smashing drinking glasses in the fireplace after consuming Vodka to ensure the toast just made will come true.

Blackberry
Duck Breasts

things you need...

4		duck breasts
½ tsp	*(2 ml)*	star anise
½ tsp	*(2 ml)*	cinnamon, ground
½ tsp	*(2 ml)*	szechwan peppercorns
½ tsp	*(2 ml)*	cloves, ground
½ tsp	*(2 ml)*	fennel seeds
½ lb	*(230 g)*	blackberries
1 tsp	*(5 ml)*	brown sugar
2		thyme sprigs
⅔ cup	*(160 ml)*	water
1 Tbsp	*(15 ml)*	**Vodka**

Soaking up the culture in Moscow's famous Red Square.

...now get cookin'

Score the skin of the duck in a diamond pattern, taking care not to cut into the flesh. Mix anise, cinnamon, peppercorns, cloves and fennel together. Rub the skin with the spice mixture and set aside while you make the pesto sauce.

Set aside 12 of the nicest looking berries for garnish.

Put the rest in a saucepan along with the sugar, thyme and water and simmer over a medium heat for 15 minutes or until the blackberries are soft.

Strain the sauce through a sieve, using a wooden spoon to get as much liquid out as possible. Discard the solids. Set aside while you cook the duck.

Heat a frying pan to medium and lay the duck skin-side down in the pan (you won't need any oil or butter).

Cook for 3 to 4 minutes then turn the breasts over and cook the other side for another 5 minutes. Turn them over again toward the end of cooking to crispen up the skin.

Cooking time will depend on the size of the breasts. Medium-rare brings out the flavor of the meat best, but you be the judge.

When cooked, set aside in a warm place to rest before carving.

To finish the sauce, pour off the fat from the frying pan and place over a high heat. Add the **Vodka** and scrape with a wooden spoon to deglaze.

Pour in the sieved sauce, stir and reheat gently.

Slice the duck breasts in thin, diagonal slices and serve with the sauce poured over.

Garnish with the fresh berries.

Serves 4   ***(facing page)***

Russians believe Vodka is best appreciated when drunk "Straight Up".

Chile's Hidden Secret

Chile is probably the skinniest looking country in the world. And though it is an integral part of the South American landmass, its shape and geometry make Chile appear like an island. But when it comes to growing grapes, that's a good thing. A very good thing!

Flanked on one side by vast Pacific waters and on the other by the awesome Andes Mountains, this pencil-thin nation stretches for more than 4,000 kilometers to where South America dips its toe into the Antarctic Ocean. Thanks to this unique geography, Chile's vineyards have been spared any serious diseases. 'Cos, believe it or not, grapes have been thriving in Chile ever since the first missionaries planted them almost 500 years ago.

Then there's the Chilean climate: blistering heat in the afternoon but very cool at night. This difference in temperature slows down the maturing process, making the grapes juicier and more flavorful.

The climate isn't the only thing unique about Chile. There's the Carmenére grape, for instance. These grapes came from the Bordeaux region of France and were likely introduced to Chile by rich landowners in the mid 19th century. Around that time, European vineyards were devastated by disease and the Carmenére grape was wiped out. But unbeknownst to the world's Wine community, it was thriving in Chile hidden among the Merlot grapes. Then, in the mid 1990s Wine experts noticed something different about the leaves.

Miracle of miracles, the long-lost Carmenére was alive and well!

Chile is not only famous for its Wines, but also for its seafood. No wonder! With all that coastline, this is a great place to find fresh fish. A favorite of the locals is grilled tuna steaks marinated in a nice Cabernet. Try adding a side of Chilean pesto with spaghetti squash and cheese. Amigos, that's excellent!

Chileans really have a lot to celebrate these days. Their Wines just keep getting better and better thanks to old vines, isolated geography and an ideal climate. Of course, Chilean hospitality will always warm the heart of any Thirsty Traveler.

Chile's unique climate is ideal for growing a ▶
wide variety of grapes.

Olives
Baked in Vino

things you need...

2 cups	*(480 ml)*	kalamata olives or other brine-cured olives, un-pitted
1 cup	*(240 ml)*	**Red Wine, dry**
¾ tsp	*(4 ml)*	fennel seeds, coarsely chopped
2		garlic cloves, thinly sliced
4 tsp	*(20 ml)*	olive oil

...now get cookin'

Preheat oven to 325°F *(160°C)*.

Combine olives, **Red Wine**, fennel seeds, garlic and oil in small baking dish.

Bake uncovered until olives are heated through, which normally takes about 20 minutes.

Serve olives warm.

Serves 4

Red Cabbage
Braised in Chilean Wine

things you need...

2 Tbsp	*(60 ml)*	butter
2½ cups	*(590 ml)*	red cabbage, thinly sliced
½ cup	*(120 ml)*	Granny Smith apple, peeled, chopped
¼ cup	*(60 ml)*	red onion, chopped
1		bacon slice, chopped
¼ cup	*(60 ml)*	**Red Wine, dry**
2 Tbsp	*(30 ml)*	red wine vinegar
½ cup	*(120 ml)*	russet potato, peeled, finely grated
1 Tbsp	*(15 ml)*	honey
		salt and pepper to taste

...now get cookin'

Melt the butter in a heavy large skillet over medium heat.

Add cabbage, apple, onion and bacon. Sauté until cabbage is crisp, about 6 minutes.

Add **Red Wine** and vinegar. Cover and cook until liquid evaporates and cabbage is tender, about 10 minutes.

Add potato and honey. Cover and cook until potato is tender, about 3 minutes.

Season cabbage mixture to taste with salt and pepper.

Serves 4

Sips & Tips
the Thirsty Traveler

For a unique Chilean Wine, look for a Carmenére. This is made from a long lost Bordeaux grape. It makes a vibrantly fruity and deeply flavored Wine.

Teriyaki
Tuna Steaks

things you need...

¾ cup	*(180 ml)*	teriyaki sauce
2 Tbsp	*(30 ml)*	soy sauce
2 Tbsp	*(30 ml)*	brown sugar
2 Tbsp	*(30 ml)*	**Red Wine**
1 Tbsp	*(15 ml)*	rice vinegar
1 tsp	*(5 ml)*	sesame oil
3		garlic cloves
2 Tbsp	*(30 ml)*	ginger root, fresh, peeled, finely chopped
2		scallions, finely chopped
pinch		hot red pepper flakes, dried
4 x 8 oz	*(250 g)*	tuna steaks, 1" *(2.5 cm)* thick

...now get cookin'

In a heavy-duty freezer bag, combine all the ingredients and then add the tuna.

Marinate covered in the refrigerator for 1 to 2 hours.

Grill on an oiled rack about 5 minutes on each side for medium-rare, or until desired doneness.

Serves 4

Some grapes are just too tempting to make it to the winery.

Sips & Tips

the **Thirsty Traveler**

The two greatest influences on Chile's climate are the vast waters of the Pacific to the west and the spectacular mountain range of the Andes down the entire eastern edge of the country.

Spaghetti Squash
in Pesto and Queso

things you need...

1		spaghetti squash, medium
¾ cup	(180 ml)	pesto sauce
½ cup	(120 ml)	mozzarella cheese, smoked or plain, shredded
¼ cup	(60 ml)	parmesan cheese, grated
2 Tbsp	(30 ml)	**Red Wine**
1		red bell pepper, slivered

...now get cookin'

Preheat oven to 350°F *(175°C)*.

Cut spaghetti squash in half and place cut side down in a casserole dish, with 1" *(2.5 cm)* of water. Bake in skin, about 30 minutes or until tender.

Scoop the meaty 'spaghetti' out of the skin and place in a large bowl. Mix in pesto, cheeses and **Red Wine**.

Mix until the cheese begins to melt. Fold in the red pepper slivers and serve.

Serves 6 to 8 **(facing page)**

Farms and vineyards in the Colchagua Valley.

Sips & Tips

The lip of a Red Wine glass is sloped inward to capture the aromas of the Wine and deliver them to your nose.

Chile Gallina
with Sun-Dried Tomatoes

things you need...

4		chicken breasts, boneless, skinless
¼ tsp	*(1 ml)*	salt
¼ tsp	*(1 ml)*	black pepper, freshly ground
⅓ cup	*(80 ml)*	flour, all purpose
⅓ cup	*(80 ml)*	olive oil
1 cup	*(240 ml)*	white onion, chopped
6		garlic cloves, thickly sliced
1¼ cups	*(300 ml)*	sun-dried tomatoes packed in olive oil, drained, coarsely chopped
½ cup	*(120 ml)*	**Red Wine, full bodied**
1 cup	*(240 ml)*	tomato sauce
1 cup	*(240 ml)*	chicken stock
1½ cups	*(360 ml)*	peas, fresh or frozen
		salt and pepper to taste
2 Tbsp	*(30 ml)*	parsley, fresh, chopped

...now get cookin'

Cut chicken breasts across the grain (widthwise) into three slices. Pound them lightly between pieces of waxed paper or plastic wrap to a thickness of ¼" *(6 mm)*. Sprinkle with salt and pepper.

Dust the chicken lightly with the flour, and shake off any excess.

In a large saucepan, heat the oil over high heat, and quickly brown the chicken on both sides, 2 to 3 minutes per side.

Remove the chicken from the heat to a platter, and cover with foil to keep warm.

Add the onion, garlic and sun-dried tomatoes to the oil in the pan. Sauté over medium-high heat until the onion is translucent and the garlic starts to brown, about 4 to 6 minutes.

Add the **Red Wine**, and sauté for 2 to 3 minutes, deglazing the pan to dislodge any browned bits from the bottom.

Add the tomato sauce and stock, and bring to a boil.

Add the peas, and simmer until the sauce is reduced by half. This takes about 10 to 12 minutes.

Add salt and pepper to taste.

Return the chicken to the sauce and cook until heated through, about 2 to 3 minutes.

Sprinkle with the parsley, and serve.

Serves 6

Sips & Tips

the Thirsty Traveler

A bottle of opened Wine stored in the refrigerator lasts 6 to 10 times longer than it would if stored at room temperature.

Santiago
Lamb

Grapes have been growing in Chile for almost 500 years.

things you need...

4 x 1 lb	*(450 g)*	lamb shanks
		salt and pepper to taste
2 Tbsp	*(30 ml)*	olive oil
1		onion, medium, coarsely chopped
1		carrot, medium, coarsely chopped
1		celery stalk, coarsely chopped
8		garlic cloves, coarsely chopped
3½ cups	*(830 ml)*	**Red Wine, full bodied**
4 cups	*(1 L)*	chicken broth
1 Tbsp	*(15 ml)*	tomato paste
2		thyme sprigs

Gremolata (topping)

3 Tbsp	*(15 ml)*	parsley, fresh, chopped
1 tsp	*(5 ml)*	lemon zest
3		garlic cloves, minced

...now get cookin'

Pat the lamb dry and season with the salt and pepper.

In a large heavy pot, heat oil over moderately-high heat until hot but not smoking.

Place the lamb in the pot and brown. Once browned transfer to a plate and set aside.

Add onion, carrot, celery and garlic to the pot and sauté until onion is softened.

Add **Red Wine** and simmer mixture, stirring occasionally, until liquid is reduced to about 3 cups *(750 ml)*.

Return lamb to the pot and stir in broth, tomato paste and thyme.

Bring liquid to a boil and simmer, covered, stirring and turning lamb occasionally, for about 1½ hours.

Simmer mixture, uncovered, stirring occasionally, 1 hour more, or until lamb is tender.

Meanwhile, in a bowl combine the parsley, lemon zest and garlic cloves. Mix well then set aside.

When the lamb is done, top with gremolata and enjoy.

Serves 4

Old Wine almost never turns to vinegar. It spoils by oxidation.

Chile Beef
Stroganoff

things you need...

2 Tbsp	*(30 ml)*	olive oil
4 x 6 oz	*(170 g)*	fillet mignon pieces, cut crosswise into ¼" *(5 mm)* thick pieces
2 Tbsp	*(30 ml)*	butter, unsalted
1½ cups	*(360 ml)*	onion, finely chopped
		salt and pepper to taste
½ lb	*(230 g)*	shiitake mushrooms, fresh, stems discarded, caps thinly sliced, about 2 cups *(480 ml)*
½ lb	*(230 g)*	white mushrooms, trimmed, thinly sliced about 2 cups *(480 ml)*
2 Tbsp	*(30 ml)*	flour, all purpose
1 cup	*(240 ml)*	**Red Wine, dry**
1½ cups	*(360 ml)*	beef broth
½ cup	*(120 g)*	sour cream
1 Tbsp	*(15 ml)*	Worcestershire sauce
8 oz	*(250 g)*	egg noodles
		chives, fresh

...now get cookin'

In a large skillet, heat the oil over moderately-high heat. Then brown beef in batches, transferring beef to a plate with a slotted spoon or tongs.

Add butter to the skillet and cook onion with salt and pepper again over moderate heat, stirring, until the onion is soft.

Add both types of mushrooms. Cook, stirring, until tender and liquid is evaporated.

Sprinkle flour over vegetables and cook, stirring for 1 minute.

Add **Red Wine**, and boil until cooking liquid has almost evaporated.

Add broth and simmer for 1 minute.

Stir in sour cream and Worcestershire sauce.

Return beef to the skillet and gently simmer, stirring occasionally, until beef is warmed through. This usually takes from 3 to 5 minutes.

Serve stroganoff with buttered egg noodles cooked according to package directions.

Garnish with chives.

Serves 4 **(facing page)**

Most of Chile's vineyards are planted with ungrafted rootstock, a rare phenomenon in modern Wine production.

Cordero (Lamb)
Pomegranate

things you need...

1 cup	*(240 ml)*	pomegranate juice, unsweetened
½ cup	*(120 ml)*	**Red Wine, dry**
2		onions, large
1		lemon, un-peeled, chopped
3		garlic cloves
1 tsp	*(5 ml)*	black pepper
1 Tbsp	*(15 ml)*	basil leaves, fresh, chopped
1 tsp	*(5 ml)*	salt
6 lb	*(2.7 kg)*	leg of lamb, boned, butterflied

...now get cookin'

In a blender, combine pomegranate juice, **Red Wine**, onions, lemon, garlic, pepper, basil and salt.

Blend until thoroughly mixed.

Rub some of marinade into the lamb. Place meat in a shallow glass pan.

Pour remaining marinade over meat. Marinate in refrigerator overnight.

When ready to cook, wipe off excess marinade.

Grill over medium coals or roast the lamb at 325°F *(160°C)* until meat thermometer reaches 145°F *(60°C)* for medium-rare.

Cover with foil and let rest 10 minutes before carving.

Serves 8

A leisurely ride through vineyards in Chile's Apalta Valley.

Sips & Tips

the Thirsty Traveler

It takes approximately five years to harvest a commercial crop from newly planted grape vines.

Winey Meatballs

things you need...

1 lb	*(450 g)*	ground beef, lean
4 to 5		scallions, finely chopped (white part and most of the green parts)
½ cup	*(120 ml)*	coarse bulgur (you can substitute rice)
1		large egg, lightly beaten
⅓ cup	*(80 ml)*	olive oil
4		garlic cloves, (2) minced, (2) coarsely chopped
1 tsp	*(5 ml)*	cumin, ground
1 cup	*(240 ml)*	parsley, fresh, finely chopped
½ tsp	*(2 ml)*	salt and pepper to taste
1		onion, large, halved lengthwise, sliced into half-moons
½ cup	*(120 ml)*	**Red Wine, dry**
2 cups	*(480 ml)*	tomatoes, canned, diced with their juice
1		cinnamon stick
½ cup	*(120 ml)*	water

...now get cookin'

In a large bowl, combine the meat, scallions, bulgur, egg, 2 Tbsp *(30 ml)* of the oil, the minced garlic, cumin, all but 2 Tbsp *(30 ml)* of the parsley and salt and pepper to taste.

Knead well, cover and refrigerate for at least 1 hour and no more than 4 hours.

Shape the meat mixture into balls, each about the size of a tablespoon. This recipe will make approximately 26 meatballs. Place on a plate, cover and refrigerate.

In a large, deep skillet, heat the remaining 3 Tbsp *(45 ml)* of oil and sauté the onion over high heat for 4 to 5 minutes or until it becomes translucent.

Add the chopped garlic and sauté for 30 seconds.

Add the **Red Wine** and simmer for one minute.

Stir in the tomatoes and cinnamon stick. Carefully add the meatballs to the skillet until the sauce almost covers them.

Add the water, bring to a boil and reduce the heat to low.

Cover and simmer for 20 minutes, or until the meatballs are cooked through and the sauce has thickened.

Remove the cinnamon stick, sprinkle with the remaining 2 Tbsp *(30 ml)* of parsley and serve.

Serves 4 to 6

Botanically, grapes are considered berries. There are about 25 million acres of grapes world-wide.

The Frontier Spirit

My old Kentucky home – there's nowhere else quite like it. Renowned for its cultural icons including Boone and bluegrass, the gloriously green 15th state of The Union is also famous for that original American spirit, Bourbon.

Old-timers in Kentucky will tell you that the early pioneers who followed celebrated American frontiersman Daniel Boone (to whom everyone in Kentucky claims to be related!) and settled there, brought two things with them – a still and a fast horse. With their strong Irish and Scottish roots, making Whiskey was a given. But back in those days Kentucky had no barley. Fortunately, there was corn, or maize, and plenty of pure, pristine water.

Voila! Corn-mash Whiskey was born.

Bourbon was named after the county in which it was produced. A major distiller of the day was a man named Jacob Spears. After filling oak casks with his corn-mash Whiskey, Spears branded the barrels with the name "Bourbon County" – a nod of thanks and respect to the French Royal Family for their support during the American War of Independence. Thus, Bourbon was christened.

To legally be Bourbon, this spirit must be aged in charred new oak barrels for a minimum of two years, be made from a mash of at least 51% corn, and be a minimum strength of 60 proof. Bourbon can also be bottled at a potent 90 proof or better! So use caution or you may find out how Mr. Boone felt when he said, "I can't say I was ever lost, but I was bewildered once for three days."

Now Bourbon isn't just your grand-daddy's drink. There's different Bourbon for different occasions and various foods. Bourbon injects an entirely new level of flavor and elegance into traditional Kentucky dishes like roast pork tenderloin and mashed sweet potatoes. And have you ever tried bread pudding or Kentucky pecan pie with Bourbon-laced whipped cream? Your taste buds will never be the same.

And that seems fitting. For as a famous Kentucky colonel once said, "Bourbon is Kentucky hospitality in a glass."

I say, I say…I'll drink to that!

Scores of Bourbon barrels sit in repose at a ▶ distillery at Frankfort, Kentucky.

Blazing
Bourbon Shrimp

things you need...

¼ **cup**	*(60 ml)*	butter, unsalted
1 lb	*(450 g)*	shrimp, peeled, deveined
¼ **cup**	*(60 ml)*	**Bourbon**
¼ **cup**	*(60 ml)*	cream
1 tsp	*(5 ml)*	tomato paste
1 Tbsp	*(15 ml)*	lemon juice
		salt and pepper to taste
¼ **cup**	*(60 ml)*	chives, minced
		pecans, salted, toasted

...now get cookin'

In a long-handled sauté pan, melt the butter and add the shrimp, sauté for 1 minute.

Add **Bourbon** and use a long-handled match to ignite the mixture, shaking the pan until the flame dies down.

With a slotted spoon, remove shrimp and place on a warm platter.

Add the cream and the tomato paste to the pan. Bring the mixture to a boil and reduce until it is thickened and coats the back of a spoon.

Add the lemon juice and season to taste with salt and pepper.

Return shrimp to pan and reheat. Add chives just before serving.

Garnish with salted, toasted pecans and serve with wild rice.

Serves 4

Bour-BQ
Sauce

things you need...

¼ **cup**	*(60 ml)*	butter
¼ **cup**	*(60 ml)*	oil, canola or corn
2		onions, medium, minced
¾ **cup**	*(180 ml)*	**Bourbon**
⅔ **cup**	*(160 ml)*	ketchup
½ **cup**	*(120 ml)*	cider vinegar
½ **cup**	*(120 ml)*	orange juice, fresh
½ **cup**	*(120 ml)*	pure maple syrup
⅓ **cup**	*(80 ml)*	dark molasses
2 Tbsp	*(30 ml)*	Worcestershire sauce
½ **tsp**	*(2 ml)*	black pepper, freshly ground
½ **tsp**	*(2 ml)*	salt

...now get cookin'

In a saucepan, melt the butter with the oil over medium heat. Add the onions and sauté for about 5 minutes or until they begin to turn golden.

Mix in the remaining ingredients, reduce heat to low, and cook the mixture until it thickens, approximately 40 minutes. Stir frequently.

Serve the sauce warm on your favorite meat.

It keeps, refrigerated, for a couple of weeks.

Makes about 3 cups (710 ml)

In 1964, the United States government finally protected the term 'Bourbon.' It also defined strict distillation guidelines for the spirit.

Tipsy Turkey

things you need...

10 lb	(4.5 kg)	turkey, cut up

Marinade

1 cup	(240 ml)	**Red Wine, dry**
½ cup	(120 ml)	**Bourbon**
½ cup	(120 ml)	**Sherry, dry**
⅓ cup	(80 ml)	soy sauce
3 Tbsp	(45 ml)	vegetable oil
2 Tbsp	(30 ml)	sugar
5		star anise, whole
1 Tbsp	(15 ml)	ginger, fresh, minced
		pepper to taste

Glaze

1¼ cups	(300 ml)	**Bourbon**
⅔ cup	(160 ml)	honey
⅔ cup	(160 ml)	ketchup
¼ cup	(60 ml)	brown sugar, packed

Premium Bourbon eases its way down the sides of the snifter.

...now get cookin'

Preheat the oven to 325°F *(160°C)*.

Have the turkey cut up as follows: drumsticks removed and cut crosswise through the bone; thighs removed and halved through the bone; breast removed (left on the bone) and each half cut into four or five pieces; wings cut at elbows, tips discarded. Reserve the backs for another use. Rinse the pieces well and pat dry.

Stir all the marinade ingredients together in a large bowl. Add the turkey pieces and coat them in the mixture. Cover, and marinate for 1 hour.

Lift the turkey pieces from the marinade, and arrange them in one or two roasting pans. Pour ½ cup *(120 ml)* of the marinade, 1 cup *(240 ml)* if using two pans, over the turkey.

Bake for 1 hour, turning and basting the pieces every 20 minutes. (If you are using two pans, rotate them after 30 minutes.)

Increase the oven temperature to 450°F *(230°C)*.

Stir the glaze ingredients together in a bowl. Brush the turkey well with the glaze, and bake 30 minutes, brushing and turning every 5 minutes. (If you are using two pans, rotate them after 15 minutes.)

Mound the turkey on a large platter, and serve. This is great hot or at room temperature.

Serves 8 to 10

Every year a Bourbon is left in the cask, 1.5% of the liquid evaporates. It is said that it then journeys to heaven and is appropriately called, "The Angels' Share".

Sips & Tips
the Thirsty Traveler

Kentucky
Lamb Skewers

things you need...

3 Tbsp	*(45 ml)*	toasted sesame or peanut oil
¼ cup	*(60 ml)*	tomato sauce (or BBQ sauce)
¼ cup	*(60 ml)*	honey
⅓ cup	*(80 ml)*	**Bourbon**
2 Tbsp	*(30 ml)*	soy sauce
1 Tbsp	*(15 ml)*	hot sauce
½ cup	*(120 ml)*	peanut butter, smooth
1 Tbsp	*(15 ml)*	lemon juice
½ Tbsp	*(7 ml)*	garlic, finely chopped
1 lb	*(450 g)*	lamb cut into ¼" x 2" *(.125 cm x 5 cm)* pieces
1		red, orange or yellow bell pepper
1		green bell pepper
12		mushrooms, whole
1		zucchini, chopped
1		red onion, chopped

...now put it together

In a food processor, add all ingredients except the meat and vegetables. Pureé until smooth, about 1 minute or less.

Cut peppers, zucchini and onion into large chunks.

Fold lamb pieces in half and place on skewer, alternating with the vegetables. If skewers are wooden, soak in water for 30 minutes.

Place in a container large enough to hold the skewers and drizzle the sauce over them covering completely, leaving ends (handles) dry.

Grill 6 to 8 minutes on each side. Alternatively cook in an oven preheated to 425°F *(220°C)* for about 15 minutes or until meat is cooked.

Serve with extra sauce you have prepared in advance (not the sauce the lamb was marinating in) on the side for additional dipping.

Serves 2 to 4   **(facing page)**

The only three living distillers with Bourbons named after them are: Elmer T. Lee, Booker Noe and Jimmy Russell.

Drunken Ribs

things you need...

4 lbs	*(2 kg)*	spare ribs
¼ cup	*(60 ml)*	**Bourbon**
¼ cup	*(60 ml)*	soy sauce
¼ cup	*(60 ml)*	brown sugar
1 Tbsp	*(15 ml)*	Dijon mustard

...now get cookin'

Preheat oven to 350°F *(175°C)*.

Place ribs in a roasting pan, cover with water, bring to a boil for 30 to 40 minutes.

When tender, remove the ribs, discard water. Place ribs on rack in the roasting pan.

Mix remaining ingredients and spread thickly over both sides of the ribs.

Roast in the oven until brown and crisp for 1¼ to 1½ hours, turning once and basting frequently with sauce.

Serves 4   **(facing page)**

My Old Kentucky home in Bardstown, Kentucky made famous by songwriter Stephen C. Foster.

Sips & Tips
the Thirsty Traveler

As Bourbon has a fruity zest, it is often included in desserts with peaches, oranges and cherries.

Louisville
Apple Ham

things you need...

8 lbs	*(3.5 kg)*	smoked ham, fully cooked, bone in
½ cup	*(120 ml)*	**Bourbon**
1½ cups	*(360 ml)*	water
½ cup	*(120 ml)*	brown sugar, light, packed
1 cup	*(240 ml)*	apple cider
¼ cup	*(60 ml)*	Dijon mustard
1 tsp	*(5 ml)*	ground pepper

...now get cookin'

Preheat oven to 325°F *(160°C)*.

Place unwrapped ham in large roasting pan. Let stand at room temperature for about 1 hour.

Skin ham and trim the fat to ¼" *(6 mm)*. Score fat on ham in a diamond pattern then cover the top of the ham with foil.

Pour ¼ cup *(60 ml)* of the **Bourbon** and all the water into the roasting pan. Bake for 30 minutes.

Meanwhile, in a small saucepan, combine remaining **Bourbon**, the sugar and ½ cup *(120 ml)* of the apple cider. Cook, stirring over medium heat until sugar is dissolved. Remove from heat. Stir in mustard and pepper.

After ham has baked for 30 minutes, remove the foil and baste with ¼ of the glaze (add water to pan if needed).

The first law office of Judge John Rowan, the original owner of My Old Kentucky Home.

Bake 1½ hours longer, basting 3 times with remaining glaze, or until internal temperature registers 140°F *(60°C)* on meat thermometer. Transfer ham to platter and tent it with foil. Let stand for 15 minutes.

Pour drippings from pan into glass bowl, skim and discard the fat. Place the same roasting pan across 2 stove top burners over medium-high heat. Add remaining apple cider, scraping up any browned bits from the bottom of the roasting pan.

Add reserved drippings and any juices from the ham on the platter. Simmer for 5 minutes. Serve the gravy over the ham.

Serves 8

In cigar pairing, a robust cigar works well with a robust Bourbon. Similarly, a mild cigar complements a smoother Bourbon.

Bourbon
Beef Tenderloin

things you need...

4 lb	*(2 kg)*	beef tenderloin
1 cup	*(240 ml)*	red wine vinegar
1 cup	*(240 ml)*	olive oil
1 cup	*(240 ml)*	**Bourbon**

...now get cookin'

Preheat oven to 500°F *(260°C)*.

Combine the red wine vinegar, oil and **Bourbon**. Massage mixture into the beef with your hands.

Marinate the beef for 1 hour.

Place marinated beef in a roasting pan, place in oven and cook for 15 minutes. Then reduce heat to 350°F *(175°C)* and cook for an additional 15 to 20 minutes. For the best results, use a meat thermometer.

Let stand for about an hour.

Place on serving platter.

Serves 4

Southern Candied
Pecans

things you need...

1 cup	*(240 ml)*	white sugar
¼ tsp	*(1 ml)*	nutmeg
¼ tsp	*(1 ml)*	cinnamon
¼ tsp	*(1 ml)*	salt
⅓ cup	*(80 ml)*	**Bourbon**
⅓ cup	*(80 ml)*	water
½ tsp	*(2 ml)*	vanilla
2 cups	*(480 ml)*	pecan halves

...now get cookin'

Cook first seven ingredients together in saucepan over medium heat until mixture reaches soft ball stage. Stir in pecan halves and spread out on wax paper to cool.

Once cooled, break up with the back of a spoon, place in bowl and serve.

Makes about 2½ cups (590 ml)

Today there is no Bourbon produced in Bourbon County, Kentucky.

Bitters is Better

They say that good things come in small packages. That's definitely the case when it comes to the lush tropical island of Trinidad and its amazing aromatic Bitters.

Located just seven miles off the coast of Venezuela, this sister island to Tobago is the spicy melting pot of the Caribbean. Here, a wealth of cultural influences, including African, Chinese, and East Indian, have washed ashore to create a sensual paradise for the Thirsty Traveler. But what do they all have in common, you ask? Bitters, baby.

Legend has it that it started centuries ago when Amerasian Indian tribes developed Bitters from a local root and used it as a medicine to aid digestion.

And bars and kitchens around the world haven't been the same since.

So just what the heck are aromatic Bitters? Other than a splash in the odd cocktail, most of us have no idea what they are, let alone how to use them. To begin with, Bitters are a select mixture of herbs and spices, collectively called botanicals. These botanicals are infused into a base alcohol, then aged for about three months. Every Bitters recipe is unique and companies producing Bitters guard their recipes like family jewels.

Take the island's oldest producer, for instance. The secret recipe for Angostura Aromatic Bitters has been locked in vaults for almost 200 years. They say that only four people know the exact ingredients, and that the recipe itself has been cut into four pieces, each locked away in separate vaults of four different banks.

Be that as it may, most Trinis know full-well that the contents of this magical little bottle and its concentrated contents enhance the taste of literally everything. Like the local Shark & Bake – a delicately seasoned shark fillet sandwiched between two golden fried pieces of bread. Or ice cream and freshly picked local fruit. Add a dash or two of Bitters and you'll experience a taste sensation unlike any other. And then there's the cocktails to accompany all that food. Whew!

So take it from the Trinis and the Thirsty Traveler – when it comes to making great cuisine even tastier, why not add a few drops of Bitters for that special secret kick.

As they say in the Caribbean, "It's better with Bitters!"

**A glorious panoramic view of ▶
Maracas Bay, Trinidad.**

Maracas Bay
Salmon Grab

things you need...

2		eggs, separated
6 oz	(170 g)	salmon, canned
		salt and pepper to taste
½ cup	(120 ml)	cracker crumbs
½ cup	(120 ml)	milk
¼ tsp	(1 ml)	**Aromatic Bitters**

...now get cookin'

Preheat oven to 325°F (160°C).

In a mixing bowl, beat the egg yolks.

Add the salmon, salt and pepper, cracker crumbs, milk and **Bitters**. Mix well.

Beat in the egg whites.

Place in a baking dish and bake in the oven for 30 minutes.

Serve either hot or cold with assorted crackers.

Serves 6

Tangy
Tomato Salsa

things you need...

4		tomatoes, large, diced
3 Tbsp	(45 ml)	lime juice
¼ tsp	(1 ml)	olive oil
1 Tbsp	(15 ml)	chili powder
2		garlic cloves, minced
1		hot pepper, seeded, diced
2 Tbsp	(30 ml)	chives, diced
1 Tbsp	(15 ml)	**Aromatic Bitters**
		salt and pepper to taste
⅓ cup	(80 ml)	cilantro, diced

...now get cookin'

Combine all of the above ingredients, except the cilantro, in a mixing bowl and blend well.

Before serving, add cilantro and enjoy with tortilla chips.

*Serves 4   **(facing page)***

The Roman Catholic archbishop's residence in Port of Spain.

Not surprisingly, Trinidad and Tobago are the heaviest users of Bitters, followed by Barbados and Australia.

Island
Pea Soup

things you need...

1 lb	*(450 g)*	yellow peas, dried
3 quarts	*(3 L)*	water
1 lb	*(450g)*	smoked bacon, chopped
2 Tbsp	*(30 ml)*	**Aromatic Bitters**
½ tsp	*(2 ml)*	salt
		parsley for garnish

...now get cookin'

Place washed peas in a bowl and cover with cold water. Let stand overnight.

Drain the peas and place in a large pot over medium heat, and add the water.

Bring to a boil. Once boiling, maintain the heat for 1 hour over low heat.

Skim off the skins of the peas as they float to the top.

Add the chopped bacon and lower the heat. Cover and continue to cook slowly for 2 hours.

Stir in the **Bitters** and salt.

Serve in individual bowls and garnish with parsley.

Serves 6

Bit O' Bitter
Curried Chicken

things you need...

4		chicken breasts, boneless, skinless, cubed
2		garlic cloves, minced
1		hot yellow pepper (West Indies red), sliced
2		tomatoes, diced
1		thyme sprig
1		chive sprig
1		onion, diced
4 Tbsp	*(60 ml)*	vegetable oil
1 tsp	*(5 ml)*	chicken flavor
3 tsp	*(15 ml)*	curry powder
4 cups	*(1 L)*	boiling water
1 tsp	*(5 ml)*	**Aromatic Bitters**

...now get cookin'

Place cubed chicken pieces into a bowl. Add garlic, pepper, tomatoes, thyme, chive and onion to the chicken. Stir to mix. Let stand for 30 minutes.

Heat oil in a skillet. Add the chicken and seasonings along with the chicken flavor to the pot. Cook for 10 minutes, gradually adding 1 cup *(240 ml)* of boiling water to the pot to prevent sticking.

Add the curry powder and the remaining 3 cups (710 ml) of boiling water.

Simmer for 30 to 35 minutes, covered.

Just before you take the pot off the stove, add a dash of **Bitters**.

Serve over rice.

Serves 4

To make a Trini Brown Cow, take 2 oz. of Mochatika, 2 oz. of cream and a healthy dash of Bitters.

Hot Tamale
Pie

things you need...

½ cup	*(120 ml)*	yellow cornmeal
1 tsp	*(5 ml)*	salt
1½ cups	*(360 ml)*	water
1½ cups	*(360 ml)*	evaporated milk
1 Tbsp	*(15 ml)*	vegetable oil
1		onion, small, chopped
1 cup	*(240 ml)*	ground beef, lean
1 cup	*(240 ml)*	tomatoes, diced
1		cayenne pepper
1 tsp	*(5 ml)*	**Aromatic Bitters**
		dash of salt

...now get cookin'

Preheat oven to 325°F *(160°C)*.

In a saucepan, mix the cornmeal, ½ tsp *(2 ml)* salt and water together. Cook over medium heat until mixture begins to thicken.

Add milk and boil for 8 to 10 minutes, stirring constantly.

In a frying pan, add oil and sauté the onion until translucent.

Add the ground beef and sauté until browned.

Add the tomato, **Bitters**, pepper and salt and ¾ of the cornmeal mixture. Sauté for 5 minutes.

Place meat into a baking dish and cover with the remaining cornmeal mixture.

Bake for 45 minutes.

Serves 4

Bombshell Bay
Shrimp

things you need...

2 lbs	*(1 kg)*	shrimp, peeled, deveined
1		lime, halved, juiced
4 Tbsp	*(60 ml)*	olive oil
1		parsley, bunch, chopped
2 tsp	*(10 ml)*	salt
1		thyme, sprig
1		garlic clove, diced
3		celery stalks, diced
2 Tbsp	*(30 ml)*	**Sherry**
1 tsp	*(5 ml)*	vinegar
1 lb	*(450 g)*	tomatoes, diced
1 tsp	*(5 ml)*	**Aromatic Bitters**

...now get cookin'

Place shrimp in a bowl of water. Squeeze lime juice into water to clean the shrimp. Remove shrimp and cut in half.

In a large skillet add the oil, and all remaining ingredients.

Cook over medium heat for 20 minutes, stirring occasionally.

Just before the mixture is done, toss in the shrimp and continue cooking until the shrimp turns pink.

Serves 6 to 8

Sugar and gentian root are the only two acknowledged ingredients in Angostura Bitters. Only four living men know the actual formula for these Bitters.

Baked
Red Snapper

things you need...

4 x 6 oz	*(170 g)*	red snapper fillets
Marinade		
2 Tbsp	*(30 ml)*	soy sauce
1 tsp	*(5 ml)*	sesame oil
Sauce		
1 tsp	*(5 ml)*	peanut oil
2		ginger, fresh, finely chopped
1		garlic clove, crushed
1		onion, small, diced
1 Tbsp	*(15 ml)*	soy sauce
1 Tbsp	*(15 ml)*	oyster sauce
1 Tbsp	*(15 ml)*	**Aromatic Bitters**

...now get cookin'

Preheat oven to 375°F *(190°C)*.

Combine the 2 Tbsp *(30 ml)* of soy sauce and the sesame oil in a bowl. Place fish in a baking pan and pour the marinade over the fish. Cover and place in the fridge for 4 hours.

Heat oil in a small saucepan over medium heat. Cook ginger, garlic and onion until tender.

Add soy sauce, oyster sauce and **Bitters**. Simmer for 1 minute.

Remove fish from the marinade and place on lightly buttered ovenproof dish. Discard the marinade.

Brush the fish with the sauce from the saucepan, retaining some for basting during cooking.

Bake for 20 to 30 minutes or until fish flakes easily with a fork. Baste regularly.

Serves 4

Trinidad
Seafood Pasta

things you need...

1¼ lbs	*(600 g)*	fettuccine pasta
2 cups	*(480 ml)*	whipping cream
2 Tbsp	*(30 ml)*	basil, fresh, chopped
2 Tbsp	*(30 ml)*	thyme, fresh, chopped
¼ tsp	*(1 ml)*	salt
1 tsp	*(5 ml)*	black pepper, ground
½ tsp	*(2 ml)*	red pepper flakes, crushed
½ tsp	*(2 ml)*	white pepper, ground
½ cup	*(120 ml)*	green onions, chopped
½ cup	*(120 ml)*	parsley, chopped
1½ cups	*(360 ml)*	baby shrimp, peeled, deveined
1½ cups	*(360 ml)*	crab
1½ cups	*(360 ml)*	clams
½ cup	*(120 ml)*	swiss cheese, grated
⅓ cup	*(80 ml)*	parmesan cheese, grated
		Aromatic Bitters

...now get cookin'

Cook pasta according to package directions.

Meanwhile, pour cream into a large skillet. Cook over medium heat, stirring constantly, until boiling.

Reduce heat and add basil, thyme, salt, peppers, green onions and parsley. Simmer for 7 to 8 minutes or until thickened.

Stir in seafood, cooking until shrimp is no longer transparent and the clams have opened.

Stir in cheeses, add a dash of **Aromatic Bitters** and blend well. Serve sauce over noodles.

Serves 4   **(facing page)**

A teaspoon of Bitters in a glass of water is said to cure an upset stomach.

Bitter
Carrot Cutlets

things you need...

1 cup	*(240 ml)*	carrots, boiled, crushed
2 cups	*(480 ml)*	rice, cooked
¼ cup	*(60 ml)*	onion, minced
2		eggs
½ cup	*(120 ml)*	milk
		salt and pepper to taste
1½ tsp	*(7 ml)*	**Aromatic Bitters**
1 cup	*(240 ml)*	bread crumbs
1 Tbsp	*(15 ml)*	vegetable oil

...now get cookin'

In a bowl, combine the carrots, rice, onions, eggs, milk, salt and pepper and **Bitters**. Mix well.

Form the mixture into cutlets.

Dip the cutlets into the breadcrumbs and set aside on a plate.

Place a frying pan over medium heat and add the oil. Dip the cutlets into the hot frying pan, cooking until both sides are brown.

Serves 8

Trini Callaloo
Trinidad's National Dish

things you need...

2 Tbsp	*(30 ml)*	vegetable oil
1		onion, medium, chopped
2		garlic cloves, minced
¼ cup	*(60 ml)*	celery, chopped
¼ cup	*(60 ml)*	chives, fresh, chopped
2 Tbsp	*(30 ml)*	thyme, fresh
10		okra, sliced
1 lb	*(450 g)*	spinach leaves, washed, coarsely chopped
1 cup	*(240 ml)*	coconut milk
4 cups	*(1 L)*	chicken stock or water
1 Tbsp	*(15 ml)*	**Aromatic Bitters**
2 Tbsp	*(30 ml)*	margarine or butter
		salt and pepper to taste

...now get cookin'

In a large heavy pot, heat oil and add onion, garlic, celery, chives and thyme. Sauté until onion is translucent.

Add okra and spinach leaves, sauté for 2 minutes.

Add coconut milk and stock. Bring to a boil then reduce heat and simmer covered for 45 minutes.

Stir in **Bitters**. Add butter, salt and pepper.

Serves 10

Angostura Bitters was invented by Dr. John Siegert in 1824 in the town of Angostura, Venezuela (now known as Ciudad Bolivar.) At the time, Dr. Siegert was acting Surgeon General of the military hospital there.

Coconut Cornmeal
Dumplings

things you need...

Dumplings

2 cups	*(480 ml)*	cornmeal
1 cup	*(240 ml)*	flour, all purpose
1		carrot, grated
¼ tsp	*(1 ml)*	salt
2 cups	*(480 ml)*	water

Coconut milk sauce

2 Tbsp	*(30 ml)*	butter
2 Tbsp	*(30 ml)*	thyme
2		pimento peppers, seeds removed, finely chopped
1		carrot, grated
4 cups	*(1 L)*	vegetable stock
8 oz	*(240 g)*	tomato paste
2 cups	*(480 ml)*	coconut milk
		Aromatic Bitters
1 cup	*(240 ml)*	evaporated milk

...now get cookin'

To make the dumplings, in a mixing bowl, place the cornmeal, flour, carrot and salt. Mix these ingredients until blended together.

Make a well in the cornmeal mixture and add water, knead until the dough is firm to the touch.

Cover the bowl with a cloth or tea towel and set aside.

To make the coconut milk sauce, in a large pot, melt the butter over medium heat.

Add the thyme, pimento peppers, carrot, stock, tomato paste, coconut milk, a dash of **Bitters** and evaporated milk. Bring to a boil. Then reduce heat to medium, place the dumplings into the pot and cover.

Cook for 15 minutes.

The dumplings will rise to the surface when they are done.

Serves 8

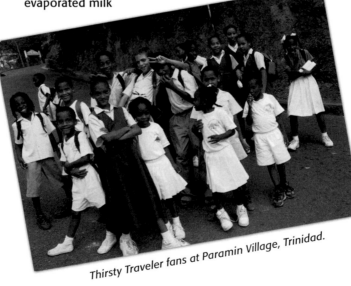

Thirsty Traveler fans at Paramin Village, Trinidad.

The news of Dr. Siegert's Bitters and its restorative properties soon spread to sea-sick sailors putting into the port. They stocked up with Bitters for the trip home.

Ports of Pleasure

Port, Porto and Portugal – the names blend together as easily as feet slide into grapes. Something the Thirsty Traveler is rather good at.

And what are those Portuguese feet so busy stomping? How about the grapes needed to produce one of the finest Wines on the planet. Port!

The Port trade is part British, part Portuguese. Britain first looked to Portugal for Wine back in the 1600s when they were at war with the French. To stabilize the Wine for the boat ride to England, merchants began adding a bucket or two of Brandy to barrels of Wine before sending them off. Thus, Port was born.

Port falls into two basic categories – those matured in wood and those matured in the bottle. Of course, within those two realms lie many variations. You've got your ruby, tawny and white Ports. And then there's the good stuff sought after by connoisseurs around the world – vintage Port.

The really good stuff is only made in exceptional growing years. Less than 2% of Port Wines ever earn vintage approval. These babies have to be tasted to be believed! Yes, they are that good.

Speaking of tasting, the best Port grapes are still crushed by foot. When machines crush the grapes, they get too mashed and this imparts a harsher taste to the end product. So stomping by foot is not only good fun, it's also good for the grapes and good for the palate. It's probably good for athlete's foot, too!

There's a Portuguese proverb that goes: "All Wine would be Port if it could." Perhaps what follows is that all recipes would use Port Wine if they could! Port adds a wonderful depth and character to many recipes. Like the classic Portuguese dish of cod poached in Port, for instance. Or bread baked with rich Port and herbs. Or maybe pears in Port sauce? Now that's a dessert worth waiting for!

If you're lucky enough to follow your nose and palate to Porto and the Douro Valley, you'll discover there's a lot more to Port than cigars and crusty old men in smoking jackets. Remember the old sailor's adage that claimed, "Any port in a storm"? Well, the Thirsty Traveler's version is, "Any Port any time!"

Picturesque Quinta de Vargellas in ▶
Portugal's Douro Valley.

Port
Cheese Spread

things you need...

10 oz	*(280 g)*	cheddar cheese, sharp, softened to room temperature, diced
⅓ cup	*(80 ml)*	**Port, Ruby**
¼ cup	*(60 ml)*	butter, unsalted, softened to room temperature
1 Tbsp	*(15 ml)*	Dijon mustard
½ tsp	*(2 ml)*	black pepper, freshly ground
¼ cup	*(60 ml)*	green onions, finely chopped
		assorted crackers

...now get cookin'

Combine the cheese, **Port**, butter, mustard and pepper in a food processor. Blend until mixture is smooth, occasionally scraping down sides of bowl.

Add the onions, using on/off turns on the processor, until blended to a spread.

Transfer the spread to a small bowl or crock.

(Can be prepared 3 days ahead. Cover and refrigerate. Bring spread to room temperature before serving.)

Place bowl of spread on platter. Surround with crackers and serve.

Makes 2 cups (480 ml)

Green
Peppercorn Sauce

things you need...

1 tsp	*(4 ml)*	butter
1 Tbsp	*(12 ml)*	peppercorn juice, jar
1½ Tbsp	*(23 ml)*	**Cognac**
2 Tbsp	*(30 ml)*	**Port, Ruby** or **Tawny**
2 Tbsp	*(30 ml)*	green peppercorns, canned, drained
2		shallots, sliced
1 Tbsp	*(12 ml)*	black peppercorns, cracked
1½ cups	*(360ml)*	beef broth
¼ cup	*(60 ml)*	sour cream
		salt to taste

...now get cookin'

In a skillet, heat the butter, peppercorn juice, **Cognac** and **Port**. Simmer on medium until there is only a tablespoon left.

Add the well-drained peppercorns, shallots and cracked black peppercorns, then the broth. Simmer and reduce to ¾ cup *(180 ml)*.

Add the sour cream and salt to taste, bring to a boil and serve with steaks.

This sauce can be made in advance and reheated just before serving

Makes 1 cup (240 ml)

At 37,672 sq. miles, Portugal is slightly smaller in area than Indiana.

White
Bordelaise

things you need...

1 Tbsp	*(15 ml)*	olive oil, extra virgin
1		onion, small, thinly sliced
4		garlic cloves, crushed
½ cup	*(120 ml)*	**Port, Ruby** or **Tawny**
1 cup	*(240 ml)*	**White Wine, dry**
½		bay leaf
2 cups	*(480 ml)*	chicken stock
1 cup	*(240 ml)*	demiglaze (can be purchased)

...now get cookin'

Heat the oil in a heavy saucepan over fairly high heat. Then reduce heat to moderate and cook onion and garlic, stirring, until onion is softened, about 2 minutes.

Add the **Port**, **White Wine** and bay leaf and boil until liquid is reduced to about 2 Tbsp *(30 ml)*, about 8 minutes.

Add the chicken stock and boil until liquid is reduced to about 1 cup *(240 ml)*, about 20 minutes. Add the demiglaze and boil, stirring occasionally, until liquid is reduced to about 1 cup *(240 ml)* again, about 10 minutes.

Pour the sauce through a fine sieve into another saucepan, pressing on and discarding solids. Keep sauce warm, covered.

Sauce may be made 2 days ahead, cooled completely uncovered and then chilled, covered.

Goes great on vegetables and meats.

Makes about 1 cup (240 ml)

Veal Scallops
Oporto

things you need...

6 Tbsp	*(90 ml)*	butter
3 Tbsp	*(45 ml)*	olive oil
1 cup	*(240 ml)*	mushrooms, sliced
8 x 6 oz	*(170 g)*	veal scallops, pounded thin
¼ tsp	*(1 ml)*	thyme
¼ tsp	*(1 ml)*	rosemary
		salt and pepper to taste
2 Tbsp	*(30 ml)*	flour
⅔ cup	*(160 ml)*	**Port**
½ cup	*(120 ml)*	whipping cream
1 Tbsp	*(15 ml)*	flour, all purpose
¼ cup	*(60 ml)*	milk

...now get cookin'

Heat the butter and oil in a fry pan. Add mushrooms and saute until golden, remove from heat.

Season the veal with thyme, rosemary, salt and pepper. Flour scallops lightly and sauté, turning to brown evenly.

Add the **Port** and cook gently for 2 minutes.

Remove meat to a hot platter.

Add the cream to the pan. Stir to scrape up brown bits and thicken lightly by combining flour and milk in a cup and adding to mixture.

Add the mushrooms and simmer for 2 minutes.

Taste for seasoning and pour over scallops.

Serves 4

Portugal produces half of the world's cork.

Pepper Salad
with Feta and Port Vinaigrette

things you need...

1 cup	*(240 ml)*	**Port, Ruby**
⅓ cup	*(80 ml)*	sherry wine vinegar
3 Tbsp	*(45 ml)*	sugar
1		cinnamon stick
¼ tsp	*(1 ml)*	nutmeg, ground
6 Tbsp	*(90 ml)*	vegetable oil
3		bell peppers, large, assorted
5 oz	*(140 g)*	salad greens, mesculin mix
¾ cup	*(180 ml)*	feta cheese (or chevres), crumbled

...now get cookin'

Preheat oven to 400°F *(205°C).*

Combine **Port**, vinegar, sugar, cinnamon stick and nutmeg in medium saucepan. Boil mixture over medium-high heat until sugar dissolves and mixture is reduced to ²/₃ cup *(160 ml),* stirring frequently, about 12 minutes.

Transfer mixture, including cinnamon stick, to a blender. With machine running, gradually add vegetable oil and blend well. Strain vinaigrette into small bowl.

Vinaigrette can be prepared 1 day ahead. Cover and refrigerate. Bring to room temperature before using.

Brush peppers with oil and place in oven until blackened, about 20 minutes. Peel and seed peppers. Cut into chunks.

Combine pepper strips, greens and feta in bowl. Toss with dressing to coat.

Divide among plates and serve.

Serves 4   ***(facing page)***

While Portugal is famous for its Port, it is also rated as the seventh largest producer of Wine in the world.

Portobello
Port Fillets

things you need...

8 x 6 oz	*(170 g)*	beef tenderloin fillets
2 Tbsp	*(30 ml)*	olive oil
1 Tbsp	*(15 ml)*	thyme, fresh, chopped
½ cup	*(120 ml)*	butter
4 x 4"	*(10 cm)*	portobello mushrooms
½ cup	*(120 ml)*	**Port**
¾ cup	*(175 ml)*	sour cream
4 oz	*(125 g)*	Stilton cheese, crumbled
		salt and pepper to taste

...now get cookin'

Rub fillets with thyme and oil and a ¼ cup *(60 ml)* of the butter. Grill to desired doneness. Keep warm in foil.

Melt the remaining ¼ cup *(60 ml)* of butter in a fry pan. Clean the mushroom tops with a damp paper towel. Trim ends and slice into pieces. Sauté for 3 to 4 minutes.

Add the **Port** and cook for 1 to 2 minutes. Stir in the sour cream and Stilton until melted, add salt and pepper to taste.

Drizzle over beef.

Serves 8   ***(facing page)***

The older section of Oporto, Portugal, retains its grandeur.

Sips & Tips
the Thirsty Traveler

Port is typically consumed as a dessert Wine and goes well with cheese.

126

Pork
with Port Glaze

things you need...

4 x 5 oz	*(140 g)*	pork loins
4		bacon slices, smoked
4		toothpicks
1½ cups	*(360 ml)*	**Port**
¼ cup	*(60 ml)*	sugar
2 Tbsp	*(30 ml)*	oil
3 Tbsp	*(45 ml)*	olive oil, extra virgin
2		garlic cloves, minced
1		shallot, medium, diced
1 cup	*(240 ml)*	pearl barley, cooked
1 oz	*(30 g)*	morel mushrooms, chopped
		salt and pepper to taste
2 Tbsp	*(30 ml)*	vegetable stock, powdered
4 cups	*(1 L)*	water

A quaintly-shaped Barca Rabelo at rest on the Douro River.

...now get cookin'

Preheat oven to 350°F *(175°C)*.

Wrap the pork loins with a piece of bacon and secure with one of the toothpicks. Place in fridge.

Pour **Port** and sugar into a heavy bottom saucepan and let simmer until reduced to a thick syrup.

Heat 1 Tbsp *(15 ml)* of oil in a frying pan and sear the loins on both sides and sprinkle with a little salt and pepper. Brush with the port syrup and place in oven for 10 minutes.

In a medium pot, heat the olive oil. Add the garlic and shallots, sauté, but don't burn. Turn down heat to medium and add barley. Stir to evenly coat barley with the oil.

Mix the powdered vegetable stock with the water and slowly start adding to the barley. Keep it at an oatmeal consistency.

Flip the pork, and brush again with the port syrup. Bake for a further 10 minutes.

Once the barley has soaked up the stock, finish it off with the chopped morels. Season with salt and pepper.

Use the remaining syrup as the sauce for the dish.

Serves 4

Vintage Port is best enjoyerd when consumed within 48 hours of opening the bottle.

Portuguese Pears
with Zabaglione

things you need...

4		pears
3½ cups	*(830 ml)*	water
1 Tbsp	*(15 ml)*	lemon juice, freshly squeezed
½ tsp	*(2 ml)*	vanilla
¾ cup	*(175 ml)*	white sugar
6		egg yolks
½ cup	*(120 ml)*	white sugar

Zabaglione Sauce

1½ cups	*(360 ml)*	**Port, Tawny (10 or 20 years old)**
1		lemon, halved, juiced
¼ tsp	*(1 ml)*	lemon rind

Caramel Sauce

¼ cup	*(60 ml)*	brown sugar
1 Tbsp	*(15 ml)*	water
¼ cup	*(60 ml)*	almonds, sliced
4		mint sprigs

...now get cookin'

Peel the pears, leaving them whole and the stalk attached.

Place pears in a shallow pan with water, lemon juice, vanilla and sugar. Cook until soft but not collapsing. This takes approximately 20 minutes. Place each pear, upright, in a small compote container made of glass and set aside.

To make the zabaglione sauce, using a double boiler, place the egg yolks and sugar in the pot, whisking until the eggs and sugar are well blended. Slowly pour in the **Port** while you continue whisking and keep doing so until you achieve a mousse-like consistency. Stir in lemon juice and rind.

To make the caramel sauce, in a saucepan, pour in sugar and add 1 Tbsp *(15 ml)* of water. Bring the mixture to a boil until it caramelizes. Color should be bronze. Be careful not to overcook.

In a frying pan, brown the almonds, quickly, careful not to burn them.

Pour the hot caramel sauce over the upright pears, and scatter the browned almonds on top of the caramel. Pour the Zabaglione Sauce around the pears and garnish with a sprig of mint on each pear.

Serves 4

Stilton or a sharp cheddar cheese is traditionally served with Port.

Apple Cider House Rules

What could be more American than hot apple pie? Well, in the New England state of Connecticut, they're making a cool case for Hard Apple Cider.

New Englanders are smart people, see. It didn't take long after the Pilgrims arrived on the Mayflower for these industrious folk to figure out the fermented juices from mashed apples makes a most excellent drink. And a deliciously potent one, too!

That's the big difference between ordinary Cider and the "hard" stuff. The former is sweet, delicious and decidedly non-alcoholic. The latter packs a punch quite worthy of the "hard" prefix. Of course, it's also the reason the Thirsty Traveler likes it so much!

Hard Cider isn't a beer nor is it a wine. It's the fermented product of the apple – a subtle difference, but a very important one. Since nearly 80% of an apple is soluble in the form of juice, Cider makers must choose their apples wisely. Most Hard Ciders are made from a mix of Romes, Roxburies and Baldwins, among others.

Ask the old-school Cider makers what apple variety they prefer, though, and the answer is likely to be the Russet. This yellowy-brown skinned baby produces just the right mix of flavor, tannins and texture for wonderful Hard Cider. It's great for cooking too.

Speaking of which, apples have been an integral part of cooking ever since the Romans figured out how to cultivate this fleshy, tasty fruit nearly 3,000 years ago.

As a rule of thumb, anything that works with Wine will work with Cider. Hard Ciders are an excellent pairing with cheese, seafood, game or poultry. Hard Ciders turn ordinary salad vinaigrettes into something special. And when it comes to creating sauces, incorporating Hard Cider into the mix is a yummy way to enhance any meal.

Throughout history, apples have symbolized luxury, fertility, love and pleasure – all the good things in life. The Thirsty Traveler believes Eve had it right! Biting into the original apple was a good thing. And so is raising a glass filled with Hard Apple Cider.

Cheers!

The Thirsty Traveler picks choice fruit for ▶ the making of Hard Apple Cider.

Smoked Sausage
Stir Fry

things you need...

1 Tbsp	*(15 ml)*	oil
1 Tbsp	*(15 ml)*	butter
2 cups	*(480 ml)*	sausage, spicy, smoked, cut into ½" *(1 cm)* slices
2		zucchini, sliced
½ cup	*(120 ml)*	green bell pepper, diced
½ cup	*(120 ml)*	red bell pepper, diced
½ cup	*(120 ml)*	yellow bell pepper, diced
1		leek, white parts only, cut into ½" *(1 cm)* cubes
1		apple, firm, buffed, cored, cut into ½" *(1 cm)* wedges, skin on
½ cup	*(120 ml)*	baby corn, canned, cut in half lengthwise
½ tsp	*(2 ml)*	cayenne pepper to taste
		salt and black pepper to taste
Sauce		
½ cup	*(125 ml)*	**Hard Cider**
1 Tbsp	*(15 ml)*	cornstarch

...now get cookin'

Heat the oil and butter in a wok or large frying pan over medium-high heat.

Add the sausage and stir fry for 5 minutes, or until browned.

Add the vegetables, apple and cayenne. Stir fry for another 5 minutes or until desired texture is achieved.

Season to taste with salt and pepper.

To make the sauce, whisk the **Cider** and cornstarch together in a cup. Pour into the wok and stir until the sauce thickens and the sausage and vegetables are coated.

Serve with rice or rice noodles.

Serves 4 **(facing page)**

To prevent apples from turning brown in a salad toss them with citrus fruits or juice.

Green Apple
Pork Chops

things you need...

¼ **cup**	(60 ml)	butter
4 x 6 oz	(170 g)	pork loin chops, boneless
1 tsp	(5 ml)	thyme, fresh, chopped
1		onion, peeled, sliced
1		garlic clove, crushed
1		green apple, cored, sliced into rings
1		red apple, cored
1 tsp	(5 ml)	white sugar
1⅛ cups	(270 ml)	**Hard Apple Cider**
		salt and pepper to taste
3 Tbsp	(45 ml)	whipping cream

...now get cookin'

Preheat oven to 375°F (190°C).

In a large heavy skillet, over medium high-heat, melt half of the butter. Fry the pork chops on both sides until a nice golden color.

Transfer the chops to a 2 quart (2 L) casserole dish with a lid and sprinkle with thyme.

Melt the remaining butter in the pan, and fry the onion and garlic until tender. Transfer them to the casserole dish.

Fry the apple rings in the pan for a few seconds on each side to give them color, then remove to the casserole dish. Sprinkle with sugar.

Spoon any excess fat from the frying pan and pour in the **Cider**.

Stir to remove any browned bits from the bottom of the fry pan. Bring the mixture to a simmer, then pour over the pork chops and apples in the dish. Season with salt and pepper.

Bake covered for 30 to 40 minutes, or until the pork chops are cooked through. Remove the pork chops and apples to a serving platter, add the cream to the juices in the casserole and stir to make sauce. Heat until just boiling.

Serve sauce over pork chops.

Serves 4

The Thirsty Traveler crew during an apple harvest.

Shaker
Roast Beef

things you need...

2 tsp	*(10 ml)*	olive oil
4 lbs	*(2 kg)*	beef eye round, trimmed
2		onions, medium, peeled, cut into 8 wedges
1 cup	*(240 ml)*	celery, sliced into ½" *(1 cm)* strips
2		garlic cloves, crushed
1 tsp	*(5 ml)*	allspice, ground
½ tsp	*(2 ml)*	ginger, ground
¼ tsp	*(1 ml)*	fresh pepper, ground
1 cup	*(240 ml)*	**Hard Apple Cider**
2 Tbsp	*(30 ml)*	molasses, dark
2 Tbsp	*(30 ml)*	cold water
2 Tbsp	*(30 ml)*	cornstarch
		salt and pepper to taste

...now get cookin'

Heat the oil in a large nonstick fry pan over medium-high heat. Add the beef and brown well on all sides.

Meanwhile, in a 4 quart *(4 L)* or larger slow cooker, combine onions, celery, garlic, allspice, ginger and pepper.

In a small bowl, mix **Cider** and molasses.

Place beef on top of onion mixture in slow cooker and pour in the **Cider** mixture.

Cover and cook at low setting until beef is tender when pierced, which takes about 9½ to 10 hrs.

Lift roast to a warm platter and keep warm. Skim and discard fat from liquid. Then whisk the cornstarch with the water in a cup and pour into cooker.

Increase cooker heat to high, cover and cook, stirring several times, until sauce is thickened, about 15 more minutes. Season with salt and pepper.

Slice beef and serve with baked or mashed potatoes or noodles.

Spoon sauce over beef.

Serves 8

There are at least 7,500 varieties of apples throughout the world.

Duck Breasts
Connecticut Style

things you need...

4 x 8 oz	*(225 g)*	duck breasts (with skin)
2 Tbsp	*(30 ml)*	vegetable oil
1		onion, peeled, sliced into thin rings
2		celery stalks, washed, diced into ½" *(1 cm)* pieces
3		carrots, peeled, cut crosswise
6		brussel sprouts, peeled
1		fennel head, medium, cleaned, diced
3		beets, peeled, cubed
5		gold potatoes, peeled, cubed
2 Tbsp	*(30 ml)*	**Hard Apple Cider**
2 Tbsp	*(30 ml)*	**Apple Schnapps (Calvados)**
¼ cup	*(60 ml)*	veal stock
1 Tbsp	*(15 ml)*	butter
		salt and pepper to taste

...now get cookin'

Season the duck breasts with salt and pepper. Then sauté them skin side down in a heated cast iron skillet on medium heat for 5 minutes each side. When the duck breasts are done to your liking (medium is usually best) place them aside.

Pour oil into a separate pan over medium heat. Add the onions and sauté for 3 to 5 minutes.

Add the celery, carrots, brussel sprouts, fennel, beets and potatoes, cover the pan and cook until tender, approximately 10 minutes. Check the pan once in a while to let the steam out.

Using the skillet the duck breasts were cooked in, discard any fat and add the **Cider** and **Schnapps**.

Over medium heat, reduce the mixture by half and add the veal stock.

Just before you are ready to serve, add the butter to the mixture. This will create a nice sauce.

Place the vegetables in the middle of a platter, slice the duck breasts in half and place them on top of the vegetables. Pour the sauce over the duck and serve.

Serves 4 ***(facing page)***

It takes at least 36 apples to create one gallon of Cider.

Arugula Salad
with Goat Cheese

Rustic Apple Tart
with Cider Jelly

things you need...

Vinaigrette

1 cup	*(240 ml)*	**Hard Apple Cider**
2 Tbsp	*(30 ml)*	apple cider vinegar
¼ cup	*(60 ml)*	apple syrup
2 Tbsp	*(30 ml)*	brown sugar, fine
¼ cup	*(60 ml)*	olive oil
		salt and pepper to taste

Salad

2		apples, peeled, sliced into thin wedges
8 oz	*(225 g)*	goat cheese, soft, crumbled
4 handfuls		arugula greens, washed

...now get cookin'

To make the vinaigrette, in a mixing bowl, add the **Cider**, vinegar, apple syrup and brown sugar and thoroughly whisk them together.

Add the oil and salt and pepper. Whisk it all together.

To make the salad, place the apples on each of 4 plates in a circular pattern.

Toss the arugula with the vinaigrette. Place the salad on top of the apple slices.

Sprinkle on the goat cheese and serve.

Serves 4

things you need...

Apple jelly

2 cups	*(480 ml)*	apple sauce, sweetened
½ cup	*(120 ml)*	**Hard Apple Cider**

Tarts

6 x 6"	*(15 cm)*	premade frozen pastry tarts, thawed
3		apples, peeled, sliced into thin wedges
1		egg, lightly beaten

...now get cookin'

To make the apple jelly, combine the apple sauce and **Cider** into a pot over medium heat and let it reduce to 1 cup *(240 ml)*. The cider should have a sauce-like consistency. Place in the refrigerator to cool.

Preheat the oven to 350ºF *(175ºC)*.

To make the tart, remove dough from foil shells. Roll the dough from each tart shell into a disc, about 6" *(15 cm)* in diameter. Place the discs on a cookie sheet.

Spread one tablespoon of apple jelly on each disc and place one or two apple slices on top of the jelly. Fold the dough over the apple slices.

Brush the tarts lightly with the beaten egg.

Bake for 13 to 15 minutes.

The tarts can be served warm or at room temperature, and taste especially yummy when you put a dollop of your favorite ice cream on top.

Serves 6

In the U.S., Cider falls into two main categories; 'Sweet Cider' and 'Hard Cider'. The Sweet refers to unfermented, while Hard is fermented and therefore contains alcohol.

Maple Glazed
Apple Rolls

things you need...

2 cups	*(480 ml)*	flour, all purpose
1½ tsp	*(7 ml)*	baking powder
1½ tsp	*(7 ml)*	baking soda
½ tsp	*(2 ml)*	salt
2 tsp	*(10 ml)*	cinnamon, ground
1		egg, lightly beaten
⅔ cup	*(160 ml)*	brown sugar, packed
½ cup	*(120 ml)*	butter, soft
⅓ cup	*(80 ml)*	maple syrup, pure
⅓ cup	*(80 ml)*	**Hard Apple Cider**
⅓ cup	*(80 ml)*	plain yogurt, non fat
3 Tbsp	*(45 ml)*	vegetable oil (preferably canola oil)

Maple Glaze

1¼ cups	*(300 ml)*	icing sugar, sifted
1 tsp	*(5 ml)*	vanilla extract, pure
1⅓ cups	*(320 ml)*	maple syrup, pure

Connecticut produces many varieties of apples, but only a select few, like these Romes, are suitable for Hard Apple Cider.

...now get cookin'

Preheat oven to 375°F *(190°C)*.

Use a Bundt pan with a nonstick cooking spray or oil. Sprinkle the inside of pan with basic white sugar, shake out excess.

In a mixing bowl, whisk together the flour, baking powder, baking soda, salt and cinnamon, then set it aside.

In another bowl, whisk together the egg, brown sugar, butter, maple syrup, **Cider**, yogurt and oil.

Add dry ingredients to egg mixture and stir until moistened. Divide the batter in half. Spoon about 2 generous tablespoonfuls of batter into each mould.

Bake 10 to 12 minutes, or until the tops spring back when touched lightly. Loosen edges and turn the cakes out onto a rack to cool.

Clean the Bundt pan, then recoat it with oil and sugar. Repeat with the remaining batter.

To make the maple glaze, combine icing sugar and vanilla in a bowl.

Gradually whisk in enough maple syrup to make a coating consistency.

Dip the underside of the cake in the glaze to coat. Set it, glazed side up, on a rack over wax paper for a few minutes until the glaze has set. For serving, break off as rolls.

Makes 2 Bundt pans full

Cider has been around for centuries and references to Cider have been found as far back as 55 BC.

Make it Schnappy!

Achtung! Could there possibly be a more German-sounding spirit than Schnapps? Ach, du lieben, I don't think so!

In the Black Forest area of southwestern Germany (actually, in every corner of Germany!) it seems everybody and their dog has their own brand of Schnapps. But just what is Schnapps? For starters, Schnapps is a generic term for a very strong, flavorful alcoholic beverage made from grain or potato-based alcohol.

Seems Schnapps got its start centuries ago when, after a major battle, a Roman emperor and his army decided to stay in and around what is now Baden-Baden and soothe their wounds in the area's natural-spring waters. In the ensuing years, the fruit seeds those Romans planted helped turn this part of modern-day Germany into one of the most productive fruit regions in all of Europe. And it is this fruit that makes great Schnapps possible!

There are actually two basic categories of Schnapps. There's Schnapps made with fruit, and Schnapps made with herbs and roots. True Schnapps has no sugar added and is definitely an acquired taste, particularly for people not used to raw distillates.

The more popular Schnapps can be fermented and distilled, whereas most liqueurs are simply fruits steeped in an alcohol that has already been fermented and distilled. This gives Schnapps an overall richer taste. And bite!

The flavor of Schnapps ranges widely, from sweet like a liqueur to dry like an infused Vodka. This marvelous diversity in taste and personality tranfers well to the kitchen. In Germany, Schnapps has been a kitchen staple for hundreds of years. And today Schnapps is part and parcel of German haute cuisine.

For instance, you could start with an entrée of grilled venison with Pear Schnapps sauce alongside some Schnapps Riesling-braised sauerkraut. Wunderbar! Or the German dessert classic, Black Forest cake soaked with Cherry Schnapps. Of course in Germany, these menu items are typically washed down with an appropriate Schnapps. Well…when in Germany!

So here's to Germany — a country whose culture, song and history are alive and well.

Ein Prosit!

Vineyards surround the ancient castle ruins ▶ above Staufen, Germany.

Pork Tenderloin
with Pear Cream Sauce

things you need...

1¼ lbs	*(600 g)*	pork tenderloin, trimmed, cut crosswise into 1" *(4 cm)* thick slices
4 Tbsp	*(60 ml)*	butter
4		Anjou pears, peeled, cored, cut into ⅓" *(8 mm)* wedges
1 tsp	*(5 ml)*	sugar
½ cup	*(120 ml)*	shallots, chopped
1¼ tsp	*(6 ml)*	thyme, fresh or dried
¼ cup	*(60 ml)*	**Pear Schnapps**
1 cup	*(240 ml)*	whipping cream
⅓ cup	*(80 ml)*	pear nectar
		salt and pepper to taste

'Barwurz', one of the many roots used n making Schnapps.

...now get cookin'

Place pork slices between plastic wrap. Pound pork slices to ¼" *(6 mm)* thickness.

Melt 2 Tbsp *(30 ml)* butter in large nonstick skillet over high heat. Add pears and sugar. Sauté until pears are tender and deep golden, about 8 minutes. Set aside.

Melt 1 Tbsp *(15 ml)* of butter in another large nonstick skillet over high heat.

Season the pork with salt and pepper.

Working in batches, add pork to skillet and sauté just until cooked through, about 2 minutes per side. Transfer to plate and cover.

Reduce heat to medium. Melt 1 Tbsp *(15 ml)* of butter in the same skillet.

Add shallots and thyme, sauté for 2 minutes.

Add the **Pear Schnapps** and boil until reduced to glaze, scraping up any browned bits, about 2 minutes.

Add cream and pear nectar. Boil until thickened to sauce consistency, about 5 minutes. Season with salt and pepper.

Reheat pears if necessary. Spoon into center of a platter. Arrange pork around pears. Pour sauce over pork.

Serve with your choice of vegetables

Serves 4   ***(facing page)***

German Schnapps can be distilled from grain, potatoes, fruits or herbs.

Schnapps
Braised Sauerkraut

things you need...

4 cups	*(1 L)*	sauerkraut, drained
1 ea		Granny Smith, McIntosh apples, peeled, cored, cut into ¼" *(6 mm)* slices
3 Tbsp	*(45 ml)*	butter, unsalted
1 cup ea	*(240 ml)*	shallots, onion, chopped
1	*(15 g)*	bacon strip, rind discarded
1 cup	*(240 ml)*	**White Wine, dry**
1 cup	*(240 ml)*	chicken broth
2 tsp	*(10 ml)*	thyme, fresh, minced
½		bay leaf
2 cups	*(480 ml)*	whipping cream
3 Tbsp	*(45 ml)*	**Apple Schnapps**
¾ tsp	*(4 ml)*	salt and pepper to taste

...now get cookin'

Preheat oven to 325°F *(160° C)*.

In a large bowl, cover sauerkraut with cold water, soak for 5 minutes. Drain in a colander, repeat.

Place a large pot over medium heat. Add butter, shallots and onion, stirring until softened, about 8 to 10 minutes. Add apples, bacon, **Wine**, broth, thyme and bay leaf and bring to a simmer. Then stir in sauerkraut.

Foil top of pot, cover with lid. Braise in oven until tender, about 1½ hours. Discard bay leaf.

Simmer cream and **Apple Schnapps** in a medium saucepan until reduced to about 1 cup *(240 ml)*, about 40 minutes.

Remove sauerkraut from oven. Add cream mixture, salt and pepper, stir well and then serve.

Serves 6

German
Gelée

things you need...

3 cups	*(710 ml)*	water
2 cups	*(480 ml)*	sugar
7 x ¼ oz	*(7 g)*	envelopes of unflavored gelatin
4 cups	*(1 L)*	**Wine, rosé**
2 Tbsp	*(30 ml)*	**Peach Schnapps**

...now get cookin'

Combine 2 cups *(480 ml)* of the water and all of the sugar in a medium saucepan and sprinkle with gelatin. Let gelatin stand 1 minute to soften.

Cook over moderate heat, gently stirring occasionally, just until sugar and gelatin are dissolved.

Remove from heat and stir in **Wine**, **Schnapps** and the remaining cup *(240 ml)* of water.

Pour into a 10 cup mould *(2.5 L)* and chill, covered, until firm. It takes about 10 hours.

Dip mould in hot water a few seconds, then invert a plate over the gelée and flip gelée onto the plate.

Makes about 8 cups (1.8 L)

In northern and eastern Germany, grain is distilled to make Schnapps. In the south, fruit and berries are the core ingredient.

Chocolate
Dipped Cherries

things you need...

2 cups	*(480 ml)*	dark sour cherries with stems
3 cups	*(710 ml)*	**Cherry Schnapps**
2 cups	*(480 ml)*	fondant
2 cups	*(480 ml)*	dark chocolate

...now get cookin'

Place the cherries in a sealed jar with the **Schnapps** and marinate for 3 months.

Once the cherries are ready, drain them in a sieve overnight to make sure that all the alcohol is removed from the surface of the cherries.

Place the fondant in a saucepan over medium heat and melt.

Dip ¾ of each cherry in the fondant. Place the dipped cherries on a wax papered tray.

Place the chocolate in a saucepan over medium heat and melt.

You will be dipping the cherries in the chocolate mixture twice.

The first time, dip, ¾ of each cherry in the chocolate, then set aside on a wax papered tray.

The second time dip the cherry in the chocolate mixture right up to the stem.

Place the chocolate covered cherries on wax paper and let rest for 24 hours.

Makes 24-30 dipped cherries

Schnappy
Apple Bundt

things you need...

½ cup	*(120 ml)*	butter
1½ cups	*(360 ml)*	apple sauce
½ cup	*(120 ml)*	**Apple Schnapps**
2½ cups	*(590 ml)*	flour
2 cups	*(480 ml)*	sugar
¼ tsp	*(1 ml)*	baking powder
1½ tsp	*(7 ml)*	baking soda
1½ tsp	*(7 ml)*	salt
¾ tsp	*(4 ml)*	cinnamon
½ tsp	*(2 ml)*	cloves
½ tsp	*(2 ml)*	allspice
2		eggs
½ cup	*(120 ml)*	nuts, chopped
1 cup	*(240 ml)*	raisins (optional)

...now get cookin'

Preheat oven to 350°F *(175°C)*.

In a medium sized bowl, using a hand mixer, cream the butter. Add the apple sauce and **Schnapps** and mix well.

Add the dry ingredients and beat for 2 minutes.

Add eggs and beat for another 2 minutes.

Stir in nuts and raisins.

Pour batter into greased and floured Bundt pan and bake for 45 to 50 minutes.

Serves 12

Schnapps is best served cold with a Beer chaser.

145

Black Forest
Cake

things you need...

1		dark chocolate cake mix (or your own from scratch)
¼ **cup**	*(60 ml)*	**Cherry Schnapps**
16 oz	*(500 g)*	cherry pie filling, canned
16 oz	*(500 g)*	whipping cream
½ **cup**	*(120 ml)*	icing sugar
2 Tbsp	*(30 ml)*	**Cherry Schnapps**
1 cup	*(240 ml)*	maraschino cherries, drained
8 oz	*(250 g)*	semi-sweet chocolate, curled

Copper stills used in making Kirschwasser.

...now get cookin'

In two 9" *(22 cm)* pans, bake cake and remove from oven as directed on the package.

Once cool, poke small holes into cakes, sprinkle or brush the **Schnapps** over both cake layers.

Thoroughly drain the cherry pie filling in a colander to remove most of the thickened juices.

Chill your electric beaters and a large bowl.

Pour the cream into the bowl and beat until the cream thickens slightly. Gradually add the icing sugar and beat until thick enough to hold its shape. Fold in 2 Tbsp *(30 ml)* of **Schnapps**.

Over waxed paper, shave the chocolate bar with a vegetable peeler, refrigerate curls until you are ready to use them.

Place one layer of the cake on a serving plate and spread its top with ½" *(1 cm)* thick layer of the cream. Spread the cherry pie filling over the cream leaving about a ½" *(1 cm)* margin around the border of the cake with no cherries.

Set other cake layer on top of the cherries and spread top and sides of the cake with the remaining cream. Shape the cream into decorative swirls on top.

With your fingers, gently press the chocolate curls into the sides of the cake.

Garnish the top with maraschino cherries, and a few remaining chocolate curls.

Serves 8   ***(facing page)***

Schnapps is a collective word meaning "Strong Spirit."

Canada's Sweet Success

What do you think of when you hear, "Niagara Falls"? Romance and honeymoons, perhaps? How about the beauty of nature? Or nutjobs and daredevils risking their lives in barrels? And now, Icewine!

Icewine is one of the world's most sought after dessert wines. And Canada's Niagara Peninsula, located an hour south of Toronto along the shores of mighty Lake Ontario, is the undisputed capital of North America's Icewine industry.

So what's the big deal about Icewine? Plenty.

Consider the geography. Lake Ontario's vast body of water creates an ecosystem all unto itself – absorbing, storing and releasing incredible amounts of heat whenever the air and land are cooler than the lake. Because of this, the Niagara region experiences moderate temperatures that help fruit mature late into the fall and early winter.

But sooner or later, you know the temperatures are going to plummet. With Icewine, though, that's good. Thanks to the lake, the temperatures can be frigid one day and relatively balmy the next. It's this temperature fluctuation that dehydrates the fruit and concentrates the sugars, acids and extracts.

Now comes the trick of harvesting those grapes – and timing is everything.

For a start, you have to wait until it's cold. But not too cold. Icewine grapes must be picked sometime after the first frost, when they've frozen into rock-hard marbles. It's then, while still frozen, that the grapes are pressed and the water is squeezed out of the skin as shards of ice. When it melts, this ice results in the highly-prized and highly-concentrated juice. It is imperative that during both the picking and pressing stages that the temperature never drops below -8° Celsius. Any colder, and there's a danger that the grapes could crack into bits during the pressing and be lost.

Because the yield from each Icewine grape is miniscule, the juice is precious. And the resulting wine is deliciously sweet and complex – making Icewine a powerful tool for cook and chef alike.

So here's to Canadian Icewine, one sweet success. Eh!

**A cold Canadian winter prepares the ▶
grapes for perfect Icewine.**

Icewine
Fromage Feuillete

things you need...

8 oz	*(225 g)*	puff pastry dough
½ cup	*(120 ml)*	whipping cream
3 oz	*(85 g)*	Roquefort cheese
3 oz	*(85 g)*	cream cheese, soft
2 Tbsp	*(30 ml)*	butter, softened
1 Tbsp	*(15 ml)*	chives or parsley, fresh, chopped
1 Tbsp	*(15 ml)*	**Icewine**
		salt and pepper to taste

...now get cookin'

Preheat oven to 375°F *(190°C)*.

Divide the dough into 3 equal portions. Roll out each piece into 3 equal strips 4" *(10 cm)* long.

Pierce each strip liberally with a fork and bake in oven for 10 to 15 minutes or until golden in color. Let cool.

Whip cream until soft peaks form.

To make the feuillete, combine Roquefort, cream cheese and butter until smooth. Add herbs, cream, **Icewine** and pepper. You may have to add a bit of salt, depending on saltiness of Roquefort.

Spread half of the mixture on 2 strips of puff pastry, stacking them on top of each other and ending with third puff pastry strip.

Using serrated knife, cut portions of feuillete and heat in oven for 3 to 4 minutes.

Serve slightly warm with chilled **Icewine**.

Serves 4

Crab
and Asparagus Salad

things you need...

¾ lb	*(340 g)*	asparagus spears, fresh
¼ cup	*(60 ml)*	mayonnaise, non fat
1 Tbsp	*(15 ml)*	lemon juice, freshly squeezed
1 tsp	*(5 ml)*	capers, chopped
½ tsp	*(2 ml)*	Dijon mustard
½ tsp	*(2 ml)*	Worcestershire sauce
1 Tbsp	*(15 ml)*	**Icewine**
12		lettuce leaves, large
¾ lb	*(340 g)*	crabmeat, fresh, drained, flaked
¼ tsp	*(1 ml)*	paprika

...now get cookin'

Snap off tough ends of asparagus. Remove scales from stalks with a vegetable peeler or knife.

Arrange asparagus in a vegetable steamer over boiling water. Cover and steam 8 minutes or until crisp tender. Plunge asparagus into ice water to stop the cooking process. Drain and chill.

In a medium bowl, mix mayonnaise, lemon juice, capers, Dijon, Worcestershire and **Icewine**.

Arrange lettuce leaves on individual serving plates and top with equal amounts of asparagus and crab. Serve each salad with 1 Tbsp *(15 ml)* dressing mixture, and sprinkle with paprika.

Serves 6   **(facing page)**

There are about 82 calories in a 2 oz. serving of Icewine.

Two Day
Summer Snapper

things you need...

4 x 8 oz	*(225 g)*	red snapper fillets, each cut crosswise in half
		salt and pepper to taste
¼ cup	*(60 ml)*	flour, all purpose
1½ cups	*(360 ml)*	olive oil
1 cup	*(240 ml)*	onions, thinly sliced
1½ tsp	*(7 ml)*	red pepper, dried, crushed
8		garlic cloves, thinly sliced
1½ Tbsp	*(22 ml)*	rosemary, dried
½ cup	*(120 ml)*	**Icewine**
3 Tbsp	*(45 ml)*	tomato juice
1½ cups	*(360 ml)*	tomatoes, plum, chopped
½ cup	*(120 ml)*	red wine vinegar
4		rosemary sprigs, fresh
24		cherry tomatoes, halved

...now get cookin'

Sprinkle fish with salt and pepper then coat with flour.

Heat ¾ cup *(175 ml)* oil in heavy large skillet over high heat.

Sauté fish in batches until golden brown, about 5 minutes per side. Transfer to paper towels to drain. Discard oil and wipe skillet.

Heat remaining ¾ cup *(175 ml)* oil in same skillet over medium high heat. Add the onions and crushed red pepper. Sauté until onions are tender, about 4 minutes.

Add garlic and dried rosemary. Sauté for another minute.

Carefully add the **Icewine** and tomato juice and simmer 2 minutes. Add the chopped tomatoes and vinegar and simmer until sauce thickens slightly, about 8 minutes.

Add the fish and simmer again, turning fish once after about 2 minutes.

Arrange fish in single layer in 13" x 9" *(3.5 L)* baking dish.

Season the sauce with salt and pepper, then pour over the fish. Cover and refrigerate at least 1 day and up to 2 days, turning fish once.

Arrange the fish and sauce on a platter.

Bring this to room temperature and garnish with rosemary and tomato halves.

Serves 8

When buying Icewine be prepared to pay top dollar. They are expensive due to the intense labor involved and the fact that the Icewine grape yields are only 10% of a regular harvest.

Chicken
in Icewine Gravy

things you need...

| 5 lb | (2.2 kg) | chicken, whole, roasting |

Marinade

2 cups	(480 ml)	**White Wine, dry**
¼ cup	(60 ml)	**Brandy**
1		carrot, grated
1		onion, grated
2		bay leaves
3		thyme sprigs
3		marjoram or parsley sprigs
4 Tbsp	(60 g)	flour, sifted
		salt and pepper to taste

Gravy

1 Tbsp	(15 ml)	flour
1 cup	(240 ml)	chicken stock
1 cup	(240 ml)	**Icewine**
		salt and pepper to taste

A wanna-be Canadian Mountie.

...now get cookin'

Preheat oven to 425° F *(220° C)*.

Wash the chicken inside and out and pat dry with paper towels.

Combine all the marinade ingredients in a large heavy-duty freezer bag set over a bowl. Add the chicken and seal the bag with as little air as possible, leaving it in the bowl. Marinate the chicken in the refrigerator for a day, turning it from time to time (the bag ensures that all of the chicken is kept moist with marinade).

Take the chicken from the marinade, pat it dry with paper towels, and sprinkle it inside and out with salt and pepper. Discard the marinade. Roast the chicken, basting often, until it sizzles and starts to brown, allowing 50 minutes to 1 hour total cooking time.

When the chicken is done, transfer it to a platter and cover it with foil to keep warm.

Discard fat from the pan, leaving behind the cooking juices. Stir in the flour and cook, stirring, for 1 minute. Add the **Icewine** and simmer for 1 to 2 minutes, stirring to dissolve the juices. Add the stock and simmer again until the gravy is slightly thickened and reduced by half.

Strain it into a saucepan, reheat it, taste, and adjust the seasoning. Serve the chicken and gravy with mashed potatoes and your favorite vegetable.

Serves 4

The correct glass in which to drink Icewine was developed by Riedel Crystal in 2000. It is narrow at the top and bottom, with a wider middle.

Icewine
Anjou Tart

things you need...

1 x 12"	(30 cm)	pastry pie shell, store bought
3		Anjou pears, peeled, cored thinly sliced
1 Tbsp	(15 ml)	white sugar
1 Tbsp	(15 ml)	flour, all purpose
1 cup	(240 ml)	**Icewine**
½ cup	(120 ml)	water
½ cup	(120ml)	sugar
2 Tbsp	(30 ml)	**Icewine**
8 scoops		ice cream, vanilla

...now get cookin'

Preheat oven to 325°F (160°C).

Defrost the pie shell.

Place pear slices, 1 Tbsp (15 ml) sugar and flour in large bowl. Toss to combine. Spoon pear mixture into center of pie shell, leaving 1½" (4 cm) border.

Bake until pears are tender, about 20 minutes.

Meanwhile, boil 1 cup (240 ml) of **Icewine**, water and ½ cup (120 ml) sugar in a medium saucepan until syrup is reduced to ½ cup (120 ml), about 10 minutes.

Drizzle half of syrup over filling. Continue baking tart until juices are bubbling thickly, about 20 minutes. Cool.

Whisk 2 Tbsp (30 ml) **Icewine** into remaining syrup.

Cut tart into wedges and drizzle with syrup. Serve with a scoop of ice cream.

Serves 8

Niagara Berries
with Sabayon

things you need...

Berries

3 cups	(710 ml)	mixed seasonal berries (i.e. strawberries, blueberries, raspberries, blackberries)
⅓ cup	(80 ml)	**Icewine**

Sabayon

3		egg yolks
2 Tbsp	(30 ml)	sugar
½ cup	(120 ml)	**Icewine**
⅔ cup	(160 ml)	whipping cream
		fresh mint or lavender
		almonds, slivered

...now get cookin'

Pour ⅓ cup (80 ml) **Icewine** over berries and place in the fridge to chill.

To make cream, in a small saucepan whisk together egg yolks, sugar and ½ cup (120 ml) of **Icewine** over low heat until thickened.

Take off heat and whisk for a few minutes until slightly cooled.

Place Icewine mixture in fridge to chill.

Whip cream until soft peaks form and fold into the cooled Icewine mixture. Return to fridge and chill for at least 30 minutes.

Place berries in individual bowls or large wine glasses. Top with a large spoonful of Icewine cream and decorate with either mint or lavender and almonds.

Serves 4 **(facing page)**

Icewine can age for up to 25 years. As Icewines age, they darken in color and also increase in price.

The BOOZE you USE...

Bitters: *A liquid flavoring combination of cloves, cinnamon, quinine, nutmeg, Rum, dried fruits and other root and herbal extracts. Used to flavor cocktails, soft drinks, as well as soups and sweet dishes, such as ice cream.*

Belgian Beer: *Lambic is a type of Wheat Beer that has the unique distinction of using unmalted wheat and is spontaneously fermented. The lambic family of Beers includes many different substyles, such as gueuze, faro, kriek and framboise. Lambic is golden yellow to light amber in color, light to medium bodied, almost flat, pungently sour, and has earthy (horsey and mousy) aromas and fruity notes.*

Bourbon: *This all-American liquor is distilled from fermented grain. Straight Bourbon is distilled from a "mash" of at least 51% corn. Blended Bourbon must contain not less than 51% straight Bourbon. Sour mash Bourbon is made by adding a portion of the old mash to help ferment each new batch, in the same way that a portion of sourdough starter is the genesis of each new batch of sourdough bread.*

Champagne: *By true definition can only be called Champagne if it comes from the province of Champagne in France. It is a sparkling Wine that's unique because it is fermented twice. The French use the 'Methode Champenoise' and that means the second fermentation happens right in the bottle.*

Cider: *The expressed juices of apples, used as a beverage or for making other products such as applejack, vinegar or apple butter. Juices that have been through the process of fermentation are known as Hard Cider.*

Gin: *There are only three styles of Gin-London, Dutch and Plymouth. The English word 'Gin' is derived from the Dutch word 'genever' meaning juniper, the original herb used by the ancient distillers to make their medicines and still the most prominent flavor in Gin.*

Icewine: *Is a late-harvest Wine. Only three varieties of vinifera grape and Vidal may be used but, usually it is made from Vidal and Riesling grapes. The grapes are left on the vine until after the first frost hits, then harvested. At the time of picking, the temperature should be - 28° F (-8°C). While the grape is still in its frozen state, it is pressed and the water is driven out as shards of ice. This leaves a highly concentrated juice, very high in acids, sugars and aromatics.*

Port: *Made mostly in Portugal and is a fortified dessert Wine. It is capable of aging in wood for much longer than most other Wines, from two years to many decades, depending on its character and potential. It may mature in cask, vat or bottle, or a combination of these.*

Red Wine (Chilean): *Soil and climate conditions in Chile can vary greatly, from one vineyard to the next. Local winemakers have learned which grapes thrive in which areas, giving rise to Wines that exhibit exceptional personality and style. Chilean Merlots and Shiraz' are amongst the most popular reds in the world.*

Rum: *Is made from sugar cane. It is a spirit that improves with age, and is aged in oak barrels that have been charred on the inside. It's these oak barrels that gives Rum its warm, golden color. Rum is mainly produced in Jamaica, Barbados and Puerto Rico.*

Schnapps: *Originated in Germany around the mountains of the Bavarian forest. The German word Schnapps is the generic term for all white (clear) Brandies distilled from fermented fruits. True Schnapps has no sugar added and is fermented from the fruit, root or herbs that will ultimately give it the flavor. This is different than many commercial Schnapps that add flavor after fermentation.*

Stout: *Is a dark Beer made using barley, water, hops, yeast and roasted malts. It has a very smooth, thick texture and it's the roasted or burnt malts that give it a dark color and a distinctive flavor. It was originally called Porter, as it was made in England and given to the dock porters. Ireland adopted it in the 1700s and gave it the name Stout.*

Tequila: *Is made from fermented and distilled sap from the heart or piña of the blue agave plant. This is a succulent, not a cactus, found in the arid highlands of Central Mexico. Archeologists say the agave has been cultivated for at least 9,000 years. Today, most of it is made in Jalisco state around the town of Tequila.*

Vodka: *Is a tasteless, odorless and colorless neutral spirit. It can come from potatoes, rye, wheat, whatever. All that matters is that the resulting mash be distilled to 95% pure ethanol, near industrial-grade alcohol with virtually no taste or smell. Russian Vodka is made of wheat and must be distilled and bottled in Russia by government regulation.*

Scotch Whisky: *There are few products that are so closely related to the land of their birth than Scotch Malt Whisky. It is the lifeblood of Scotland, historically, socially and economically. It is made from only the most elemental Scottish ingredients; water and malted barley. On the island of Islay, where a number of Scottish distilleries are located, peat is said to be the key ingredient.*

White Wine (Californian): *Sonoma County, California, produces unique whites. The valley's fog-cooled climate and well-drained soils contribute to the grape formation and production of these Wines. Early-ripening varieties of Chardonnay and Pinot Noir thrive in this distinctive climate, as do Zinfandel and grapes for sparkling Wines.*

Glossary of Culinary Terms

Aging: *A term used to describe the holding of meats at a temperature of 34° to 36°F (4° to 5°C). for a period of time to break down the tough connective tissues through the action of enzymes.*

Al Dente: *Meaning "to the teeth". Used to describe the correct degree of cooking for pasta and vegetables. This is not exactly a procedure, but a sensory evaluation for deciding when the food is finished cooking.*

Allspice: *A single spice whose flavor is reminiscent of a blend of nutmeg, cloves, juniper berries, pepper and cinnamon. It is processed from the fruit of an evergreen tree found in the Western Hemisphere.*

Bake: *To cook by dry heat, either covered or uncovered, in an oven or oven-type appliance.*

Barbecue: *To cook over an open fire or on a spit, or in an oven, usually basting with a savory sauce.*

Baste: *To moisten food as it cooks, with pan drippings, fruit juice, butter, or a sauce. Prevents the drying of the food and adds flavor.*

Béarnaise: *(French) Sauce derived from Hollandaise, with a tarragon reduction added.*

Beat: *To make a mixture smooth by introducing air with a brisk over and over motion using a spoon, or a rotary motion using an egg beater (whisk) or an electric beater.*

Beurre Manie: *Literally, handled butter. It is an equal mixture of soft butter and flour, used for thickening soups and sauces.*

Black Bean: *A relatively large, dried bean with black skin, cream-colored flesh and a sweet flavor. Also called a turtle bean.*

Black-Eyed Pea: *A member of the pea family native to China; small and beige with a black circular eye on the curved edge and used in southern U.S. and Chinese cuisines. Also known as a cow pea.*

Blanch: *To place food in boiling water briefly either to partially cook them or to aid in the removal of skin (e.g. nuts, peaches, tomatoes). Blanching also removes the bitterness from citrus zests.*

Blend: *To combine two or more ingredients thoroughly.*

Boil: *To cook in boiling liquid in which bubbles rise vigorously to the surface. The boiling point of water is 212°F (100°C).*

Bok Choy: *A Chinese cabbage with white stems and broad, dark green leaves. Shanghai or baby bok choy is smaller and has a more delicate flavor. Choose stalks that are crisp with unblemished leaves.*

Bordelaise: *Describes a brown sauce that includes shallots and red wine. Some versions of this sauce include slices of bone marrow added at the end of cooking.*

Braise: *A cooking method where food (usually meat) is first browned in oil, then cooked slowly in a liquid (Wine, stock or water).*

Brine: *A solution of salt and water used in pickling. Brine draws natural sugars and moisture from foods and forms lactic acids which protects them against spoilage.*

Calvados: *An Apple Brandy from Normandy, France, made from Cider that has been aged for up to two years and distilled.*

Caper: *The small buds of a Mediterranean shrub. They are usually pickled in vinegar or dried and salted.*

Caramelize: *To melt sugar, slowly over low heat without burning, until it melts and becomes brown in color.*

Carpaccio: *Originally, paper thin slices of raw beef with a sauce of olive oil and parmesan cheese, invented at Harry's Bar in Venice. In recent years, the term has come to describe very thinly sliced vegetables, raw or smoked meats and fish.*

Cayenne Pepper: *A hot pungent peppery powder blended from various ground dried hot chiles and salt, has a bright orange-red color and fine texture; also known as red pepper and usually used ground.*

Chop: *To cut into pieces of roughly the same size, either small (finely chopped) or larger (coarsely chopped).*

Cilantro: *Also known as Coriander and Chinese parsley. It resembles and is often used like parsley. The seeds of this aromatic plant are often dried and used as a spice.*

Cloves: *The brown, hard dried flower buds of an aromatic Southeast Asian evergreen. They are useful in both whole and ground forms.*

Coconut Milk: *Is made by combining equal parts water and shredded fresh or desiccated coconut meat and simmering until foamy, then strained, squeezing as much of the liquid as possible from the coconut meat. The coconut meat can be combined with water again for a second, diluted batch of coconut milk.*

Coddle: *To gently poach in barely simmering liquid.*

Icing Sugar: *Refined sugar ground into a fine, white, easily dissolved powder.*

Consommé: *A clarified broth or stock.*

Core: *To remove the central seeded area from a fruit or vegetable.*

Couscous: *A grain-like hard wheat semolina that has been ground, moistened, and rolled in flour. The grain is then steamed (for 40 min.) and traditionally served with a stew. The couscous you find in most American grocery (usually in the rice aisle) stores is precooked.*

Cream (as in butter and sugar): *Thoroughly beating butter in a bowl, then gradually adding sugar until mixture is fluffy and creamy.*

Cube: *To cut food into small cube shapes, larger than diced, usually about ½" (.5 cm).*

Cumin: *An Indian spice with an earthy flavor, also known as comino and usually appears in ground form or as a seed. Cumin is featured in Middle Eastern and Latin American cuisines.*

Dash: *A very small amount, less than $^1/_8$ tsp (.5 ml).*

Deglaze: *To add liquid such as Wine, stock or water to the bottom of a pan to dissolve the caramelized drippings so that they may be added to a sauce, for added flavor.*

Demiglace: *A thick, intensely flavored, glossy brown sauce. Made, by thickening a rich veal stock, enriching it with diced vegetables, tomato paste and Madeira or Sherry, then reducing it until concentrated.*

Devein: *To remove the blackish vein from the back of a shrimp using a special utensil called a deveiner or with the tip of a sharp knife.*

Dice: *To cut a solid into cubes of $^1/_8$" to ¼" (.125 cm to .25 cm).*

Dutch Oven: *A heavy cooking pot usually of cast iron or enamel-on-iron, with a heavy cover.*

Fennel: *A perennial plant with feathery foliage and tiny flowers. The oval, green-brown seeds have prominent ridges, short, hair-like fibers and a weak, anise-like flavor and aroma. Available whole and ground.*

Feta: *A soft Greek cheese made from ewe's milk (or occasionally, goat's milk) and pickled in brine. Has a white color, crumbly texture and salty, sour, tangy flavor.*

Fillet: *A piece of meat, poultry or fish without bones.*

Five-spice Powder: *A fragrant, pungent, slightly sweet and hot Chinese spice mixture. The blend traditionally includes star anise, cinnamon, Szechwan peppercorns, cloves and fennel.*

Flambé: *To flame, using alcohol as the burning agent; flame causes caramelization, enhancing flavor.*

Florets: *(florettes) The small, closely-clustered "flowering" part of a food, such as broccoli or cauliflower.*

Fold: *To gently combine two ingredients, using a bottom-to-top motion with a spoon or scraper.*

Fondant: *An icing made of sugar syrup and glucose, which is cooked to a specific temperature and then kneaded to a smooth, soft paste. This paste can then be colored or flavored and used as icing for cakes and petit fours.*

Garnish: *The small decoration or artistic edible complement. It is added to finish a dish or platter to make the food more appealing to the eye.*

Glaze: *Any shiny coating applied to a food or created by browning.*

Grease: *To rub the inside of baking pans with butter, margarine or baking sprays to prevent from sticking.*

Hollandaise: *A sauce made of butter, egg and lemon juice or vinegar.*

Jalapeno: *A small green chile pepper that is mildly hot. Serrano peppers are a good substitute.*

Jerk: *A fiery Jamaican seasoning blend used in the preparation of grilled foods, especially pork or chicken. It usually includes chilies, thyme, allspice, garlic and onions.*

Julienne: *To cut vegetables in finger-length, narrow strips.*

Maple Syrup: *A reddish-brown, viscous liquid with a sweet distinctive flavor, made by reducing the sap of the North American maple tree.*

Marinate: *Soak in a liquid containing an acid such as lemon juice, vinegar or Wine, plus seasonings and sometimes oil. Used to flavor and tenderize meat, fish and poultry. The liquid is called a marinade.*

Mascapone: *A rich triple cream, fresh cheese from Italy with a texture resembling that of solidified whipped cream.*

Meat Thermometer: *Recommended to use when cooking pork, beef, lamb and fowl. Use the following temperatures as a guideline. Note, when inserting into meat, keep away from any bone:*

> *rare: 125°F (53°C)*
> *medium: 135°F (58°C)*
> *well done: 145°F (63°C)*

Mince: *To grind or chop into very fine pieces.*

Parchment Paper: *A silicon based paper that can withstand high heat and keeps food from sticking. Parchment paper can often be reused several times.*

Poach: *To cook in liquid held below the boiling point.*

Portobello Mushroom: *A full-grown portobello mushroom can easily measure 6" in diameter. They have an earthy meaty flavor.*

Purée: *The process of mashing a food to a fine pulp in a blender or food processor.*

Ramekin: *A small shallow baking dish or porcelain cups, often used to make soufflés. The foods cooked in these are also served in them.*

Reduce: *(reduction) The process of rapid boiling in an uncovered pan, then simmering the liquid until it decreases in volume through evaporation. Used to increase the flavor of a liquid.*

Rice Vinegar: *Is made from fermented rice and comes in several varieties, each differing in intensity and tartness.*

Risotto: *An Italian dish made by gradually adding hot stock to starchy short-grained (Arborio) rice, stirring constantly until the rice is cooked and creamy.*

Roasted Garlic: *Cut the top third of the garlic head off and discard it. Drizzle the remainder with olive oil and put it in aluminum foil. Bake in a 400°F (204°C) oven until edges of the garlic are caramelized (about 40 min.).*

Roux: *A combination of 50% fat and 50% flour cooked together to form a smooth paste. Roux is used as a thickening agent in cooking liquids such as soups and sauces.*

Sabayon: *A frothy custard of egg yolk, sugar and Wine that is made by whisking the ingredients over simmering water.*

Saffron: *Dried, yellow-orange stamens of the flower of crocus sativus and is available as threads and as grains. The threads are considered best, though far more expensive.*

Sauté: *To cook food quickly in a small amount of preheated fat or oil, until brown, in a skillet or sauté pan over direct heat.*

Savory: *A term used to refer to foods that are the opposite of sweet.*

Score: *To cut shallow slits at regular intervals on the surface of a food. As in scoring fat on ham before glazing, for either decoration or to tenderize, or to prevent edges from curling.*

Sear: *The process of sealing the surface of foods by cooking it briefly in a small amount of extremely hot fat, or on a very hot grill.*

Semifreddo: *Meaning "half cold", this is gelato with whipped cream folded into it.*

Shallots: *An onion variety that produces clusters of bulbs. Their flavor is slightly less intense than that of onions.*

Shiitake Mushroom: *A strongly flavored mushroom used in both its fresh and dried form. Also called Chinese, black or Oriental mushroom in its dried form.*

Sieve: *To strain liquid from food through the fine mesh or perforated holes of a strainer or sieve.*

Simmer: *To cook in liquid just below the boiling point; bubbles form slowly and burst before reaching surface.*

Slice: *To cut food into thin sections using a sharp knife.*

Sliver: *To cut into long thin pieces with a knife.*

Star Anise: *A star-shaped spice used in Oriental cooking. It is used by some as a substitute for the bay leaf.*

Steam: *To cook indirectly by setting food on top of boiling water in a covered pot.*

Thicken: *The process of making a liquid substance dense by adding a thickening agent (e.g. flour, gelatin, corn starch) or by cooking to evaporate some of the liquid.*

To Taste: *To add an ingredient, such as salt and pepper, to a recipe in an amount which indicates the personal preference of the cook.*

Toss: *To mix salad ingredients lightly with a rising and falling action.*

Vinaigrette: *A cold sauce of oil and vinegar flavored with seasonings; served with cold meats or vegetables or as a dressing with salad greens.*

Whip: *The process of beating liquids or semi-liquids vigorously in order to incorporate air, and ultimately volume, into the product.*

Whisk: *A mixing tool designed so its many strands of looped wire make it effective for beating. To beat with a whisk until well mixed.*

Zest: *The rind of the fruit contains oils that lend a nice flavor to the final dish. When zesting, be careful NOT to include the white pith, as that adds a bitter taste.*

Index